500 BRAND AND MARKETING DEFINITIONS

For reserchers and professionals

AUTHORS:
    Pedro Manuel do Espírito Santo (+351) 935 605 391
      (eng.espirito.santo@gmail.com)
    Patrícia Milene Azinheira Cardoso (+351) 966 345 385
      (patricia.milene.cardoso@gmail.com)

Title: 500 BRAND AND MARKETING DEFINITIONS, For researchers and professionals
Independently published

Copyright © 2021
  Pedro Espírito Santo
  Patricia Cardoso

All rights reserved. This publication may not be reproduced or transmitted, in whole or in part, by any electronic or mechanical means, photocopying, scanning, recording, information storage and retrieval system, website, blog, or otherwise, without prior written permission from the authors of this book.

Marketing and brand management are concepts that have greater importance in the management of organizations since the end of the 20th century. Over the past few years, there have been many concepts related to brand management that researchers have studied and managers have applied in their companies.

In this context, this book is an important contribution for researchers and managers because it presents the concepts about brand management that had been studied by researchers and brand managers will be able to apply in their companies.

The book "500 Brand and Marketing Definitions for Researchers and Professionals" is the result of a definition search found in scientific papers, with an emphasis on the definitions that have been applied in recent years.

We identified more than 500 brand definitions studied in the main scientific journals.

The definitions presented in this book focused on studies on brand management and concepts related to these investigations.

Therefore, "500 Brand and Marketing Definitions for Researchers and Professionals" present the concepts and their bibliographic source. Thus, we consider that the concepts presented are more up-to-date and applicable.

Therefore, the book "500 Definitions of Branding and Marketing Researchers and for Professionals" is an indispensable book for people who work in brand and marketing management.

Pedro Espírito Santo & Patrícia Cardoso

DEFINITIONS

Activation

Definition: Activation involves a customer's level of energy, efort and time spent on a brand in a particular consumer-brand interaction. It represents the behavioural dimension of customer brand engagement.

> **Source:** Nyadzayo, M. W., Leckie, C. & Johnson, L. W. (2020). The impact of relational drivers on customer brand engagement and brand outcomes. *Journal of Brand Management*, 27(5), 561-578.

Active brand logo

Definition: Active brand logo designs are logos that give the impression of motion.

> **Source:** Baxter, S. M. & Ilicic, J. (2018). May the force drag your dynamic logo: The brand work-energy effect. *International Journal of Research in Marketing*, 35(3), 509-523.

Active brand personality

Definition: Active brand personality refers to an personality with three characteristics: active, dynamic, and innovative.

> **Source:** Molinillo, S., Japutra, A., Nguyen, B. & Chen Cheng-Hao, S. (2017). Responsible brands vs active brands? An examination of brand personality on brand awareness, brand trust, and brand loyalty. *Marketing Intelligence & Planning*, 35(2), 166-179.

Active engagement

Definition: Active engagement refers to the strongest level of brand loyalty. This occurs when customers are willing to invest time, energy, money, or other resources in the brand beyond those expended during the purchase or consumption of the brand.

> **Source:** Shim, C., Kang, S., Kim, I. & Hyun, S. S. (2017). Luxury-cruise travellers' brand community perception and its consequences. *Current Issues in Tourism*, 20(14), 1489-1509.

Actual self

Definition: Actual self reflects the present perceived reality of a customer by himself (i.e., who I am).

> **Source:** Kim, Y.-K. & Sullivan, P. (2019). Emotional branding speaks to consumers' heart: the case of fashion brands. *Fashion and Textiles*, 6(1), 2.

Ad skepticism

Definition: Ad skepticism is defined as the tendency to disbelieve advertising claims.

> **Source:** Kang, J. (2020). The Effect of Ad Skepticism and Celebrity Preference on Brand Attitude Change in Celebrity-Endorsed Advertising. *Japanese Psychological Research*, 62(1), 26-38.

Aesthetic

Definition (1): Aesthetic is a function of how well a design aligns with the segment average. Aesthetic is a joint function of an object's visual typicality and the categorization structures retrieved from memory

> **Source:** Heitmann, M., Landwehr, J. R., Schreiner, T. F. & van Heerde, H. J. (2020). Leveraging Brand Equity for Effective Visual Product Design. *Journal of Marketing Research*, 57(2), 257-277.

Definition (2): Aesthetic is related with the desire for beauty and relate it to the use of elements such as line, form, colour, texture, and pattern to create a pleasing design.

> **Source:** Hwang, C. & Kim, T. H. (2020) Muslim Women's Purchasing Behaviors Toward Modest Activewear in the United States. *Clothing and Textiles Research Journal*

Aesthetic labor fit perceptions

Definition: Aesthetic labor fit perceptions are defined as the extent to which various aspects of employee aesthetics in a service encounter are perceived as a cohesive and consistent reflection of the brand.

> **Source:** Wu, L., King, C. A., Lu, L. & Guchait, P. (2020). Hospitality aesthetic labor management: Consumers' and prospective employees' perspectives of hospitality brands. *International Journal of Hospitality Management*, 87, 102373.

Aesthetically appealing

Definition: Aesthetically appealing occurs when a brand has a good-looking, visually attractive and pleasing appearance.

> **Source:** Warren, C., Batra, R., Loureiro, S. M. C. & Bagozzi, R. P. (2019). Brand Coolness. *Journal of Marketing*, 83(5), 36-56.

Affect

Definition: Affect is known as a complex state of the organism, involving bodily changes of widespread character-in breathing, pulse, gland secretion, etc.- and, on the mental side, a state of excitement or perturbation, marked by strong feeling.

> **Source:** Han, H., Nguyen, H. N., Song, H., Chua, B.-L., Lee, S. & Kim, W. (2018). Drivers of brand loyalty in the chain coffee shop industry. *International Journal of Hospitality Management*, 72, 86-97.

Affection

Definition: Affection describes a customer's degree of positive brand-related affect in a specific customer-brand interaction.

> **Source** Nyadzayo, M. W., Leckie, C. & Johnson, L. W. (2020). The impact of relational drivers on customer brand engagement and brand outcomes. *Journal of Brand Management*, 27(5), 561-578.

Affective brand trust

Definition: Affective brand trust is defined as a belief generated on the levels of care and concern that the brand exhibits. Emotional trust is the main principle of this dimension of brand trust.

> **Source:** Srivastava, N., Dash Satya, B. & Mookerjee, A. (2015). Antecedents and moderators of brand trust in the context of baby care toiletries. *Journal of Consumer Marketing*, 32(5), 328-340.

Affective experience

Definition: Affective experience is associated with explicit emotional responses that can be positive (e.g., love, desire, and pride) or negative (e.g., fear, disgust, and despair).

> **Source:** Kang, J. (2020). The Effect of Ad Skepticism and Celebrity Preference on Brand Attitude Change in Celebrity-Endorsed Advertising. *Japanese Psychological Research*, 62(1), 26-38.

Affective orientation

Definition: Affective orientation is defined as the tendency to use affect as information. This orientation argues that affection-oriented individuals recognize small changes in their emotional states.

> **Source:** Kao Danny, T. & Wu, P.-H. (2019). The impact of affective orientation on bank preference as moderated by cognitive load and brand story style. *International Journal of Bank Marketing*, 37(5), 1334-1349.

Agreeableness

Definition: Agreeableness is a personality trait which is characterized as soft-hearted, good-natured, trusting, helpful, forgiving, gullible, and straightforward.

> **Source:** Vashist, D. (2018). Effect of product involvement and brand prominence on advergamers' brand recall and brand attitude in an emerging market context. *Asia Pacific Journal of Marketing and Logistics*, 30(1), 43-61.

Altruism

Definition (1): Altruism is about acting on others' behalf without expecting any benefit. Consumers with higher levels of altruism are more cautious about the ecological benefits of their behaviour than the consequences for their own selves.

> **Source:** Panda, T. K., Kumar, A., Jakhar, S., Luthra, S., Garza-Reyes, J. A., Kazancoglu, I. & Nayak, S. S. (2020). Social and environmental sustainability model on consumers' altruism, green purchase intention, green brand loyalty and evangelism. *Journal of Cleaner Production, 243*, 118575.

Definition (2): Altruism demonstrates people's enjoyment in helping others without expecting anything in return.

> **Source:** Chang, Y., Hou, R.-J., Wang, K., Cui, A. P. & Zhang, C.-B. (2020). Effects of intrinsic and extrinsic motivation on social loafing in online travel communities. *Computers in Human Behavior, 109*, 106360.

Definition (3): An individual with altruism is someone who is willing to help others without expecting anything in return and social benefit is associated with individuals' needs for recognition and social support.

> **Source:** Pan, L.-Y., Huang, H.-C. & Ko, C.-H. (2020). A prideful posting a day keeps admiring readers awake: voluntary bloggers in a self-construal framework. *Behaviour & Information Technology*, 1-16.

Ambassador behaviors

Definition: Ambassador behaviors are defined as individual behaviors which are consistent with the brand image and brand values.

> **Source:** Chen, N. & Dwyer, L. (2018). Residents' Place Satisfaction and Place Attachment on Destination Brand-Building Behaviors: Conceptual and Empirical Differentiation. *Journal of Travel Research, 57*(8), 1026-1041.

Animosity

Definition: Animosity can be defined as remnants of antipathy related to the brand through behaviors.

> **Source:** Dimitriu, R. & Guesalaga, R. (2017). Consumers' Social Media Brand Behaviors: Uncovering Underlying Motivators and Deriving Meaningful Consumer Segments. *Psychology & Marketing, 34*(5), 580-592.

Anthropomorphism

Definition: Anthropomorphism refers to the attribution of humanlike characteristics, motivations, intentions, and emotions to nonhuman entities (e.g. Brands, objects).

> **Source:** Portal, S., Abratt, R. & Bendixen, M. (2018). Building a human brand: Brand anthropomorphism unravelled. *Business Horizons, 61*(3), 367-374.

Artificial intelligence

Definition: Artificial intelligence is refered as a field of science and engineering concerned with the computational understanding of what is commonly called intelligent behaviour, and with the creation of artefacts which exhibit such behaviour."

> **Source:** Trivedi, J. (2019). Examining the Customer Experience of Using Banking Chatbots and Its Impact on Brand Love: The Moderating Role of Perceived Risk. *Journal of Internet Commerce, 18*(1), 91-111.

Attachment

Definition (1): Attachment is defined as the bond connecting a person with the brand.

> **Source:** Sugitani, Y. (2018). The Effect of Self- and Public-Based Evaluations on Brand Purchasing: The Interplay of Independent and Interdependent Self-Construal. *Journal of International Consumer Marketing, 30*(4), 235-243.

Definition (2): Attachment is an emotion-laden target-specific bond between an individual and a specific object.

> **Source:** Bian, X. & Haque, S. (2020). Counterfeit versus original patronage: Do emotional brand attachment, brand involvement, and past experience matter? *Journal of Brand Management, 27*(4), 438-451.

Attitude

Definition (1): Attitude is defined as a learned predisposition to respond in a consistently favorable or unfavorable manner with respect to a given object or a specific brand.

> **Source:** Schade, M., Hegner, S., Horstmann, F. & Brinkmann, N. (2016). The impact of attitude functions on luxury brand consumption: An age-based group comparison. *Journal of Business Research, 69*(1), 314-322.

Definition (2): Attitude is a term that includes one's beliefs, feelings, perceptions and actions. Attitude is a lasting general evaluation of people, objects and issues. It is also defined as a salient belief toward a certain behavior and the evaluation of that.

> **Source:** Abalkhail, T. S. (2018). The Attitudes of Saudi Youth Toward U.S. Apparel Brand Names. *Journal of International Consumer Marketing, 30*(1), 58-68

Definition (3): Attitude is defined as individuals' positive or negative feelings associated with conducting a particular behavior . Attitude is considered a function of salient beliefs, which may be formed by observation, secondary information, or by an inferential method.

> **Source:** Bianchi, C., Milberg, S. & Cúneo, A. (2017). Understanding travelers' intentions to visit a short versus long-haul emerging vacation destination: The case of Chile. *Tourism Management, 59*, 312-324.

Definition (4): Attitude is defined as an individual's personal evaluation, emotional feelings, and actions tendency towards activities, objects, ideas, and behaviours. This concept acts as a basis to individual's willingness in behaving under a specific manner.

> **Source:** Cuomo, M., Foroudi, P., Tortora, D., Hussain, S. & Melewar, T. C. (2019). Celebrity Endorsement and the Attitude Towards Luxury Brands for Sustainable Consumption. *Sustainability*, *11*, 6791.

Definition (5): Attitude an be defined as an individual's assessment or opinion of people's objects, advertisements or issues.

> **Source:** Min, J. H. J., Chang, H. J. J., Jai, T.-M. C. & Ziegler, M. (2019). The effects of celebrity-brand congruence and publicity on consumer attitudes and buying behavior. *Fashion and Textiles*, *6*(1).

Attitude toward a brand

Definition: Attitude toward a brand corresponds to consumers' assessment of the brand as a set of cumulative associations and beliefs which impacts on brand trust and reputation.

> **Source:** Foroudi, P. (2019). Influence of brand signature, brand awareness, brand attitude, brand reputation on hotel industry's brand performance. *International Journal of Hospitality Management*, *76*, 271-285.

Attitudes toward foreign products

Definition: Attitude toward foreign products is defined as a process whereby people learn cultural norms and values that differ from their native values.

> **Source** Abalkhail, T. S. (2018). The Attitudes of Saudi Youth Toward U.S. Apparel Brand Names. *Journal of International Consumer Marketing*, *30*(1), 58-68.

Attitudinal loyalty

Definition (1): Attitudinal loyalty suggests the emotional and psychological longing of the customer to repurchase and to recommend to other people.

> **Source:** Agyei, J., Sun, S., Abrokwah, E., Penney, E. K. & Ofori-Boafo, R. (2020). Influence of Trust on Customer Engagement: Empirical Evidence From the Insurance Industry in Ghana. *SAGE Open*, *10*(1).

Definition (2): Attitudinal loyalty is related with the predisposition of buyers to maintain an ongoing relationship with the seller.

> **Source:** Ramaswami, S. N. & Arunachalam, S. (2016). Divided attitudinal loyalty and customer value: role of dealers in an indirect channel. Journal of the Academy of Marketing Science, 44(6), 770-790

Attribution theory
Definition: Attribution theory refers to the perception or inference of cause, how individuals may succeed or fail in dynamic interactions with brands, and what causes inferences about a particular behavior.

> **Source:** Foroudi, P. (2019). Influence of brand signature, brand awareness, brand attitude, brand reputation on hotel industry's brand performance. *International Journal of Hospitality Management*, 76, 271-285.

Authentic brand
Definition: Authentic brand is defined as a brand behave in a way that is consistent with or true to its perceived essence or roots.

> **Source:** Warren, C., Batra, R., Loureiro, S. M. C. & Bagozzi, R. P. (2019). Brand Coolness. *Journal of Marketing*, 83(5), 36-56.

Autobiographical memories
Definition: Autobiographical memories are reminiscences of past episodes from one's own life experiences.

> **Source:** Mandal, S. (2020). Employing autobiographical memory perspective to influence self-congruence and brand preference. *Journal of Consumer Behaviour*, 19(5), 481-492.

B2B brand
Definition: B2B brand is defined as a brand that deals in business-to-business (for more details see the brand definition).

> **Source:** Zhang, J., Jiang, Y., Shabbir, R. & Zhu, M. (2016). How brand orientation impacts B2B service brand equity? An empirical study among Chinese firms. *Journal of Business & Industrial Marketing*, 31(1), 83-98.

Behavioral brand loyalty
Definition: Behavioral brand loyalty is defined as a customer's behavior toward a specific brand in terms of repeat purchasing patterns.

> **Source:** Mody, M. & Hanks, L. (2020). Consumption Authenticity in the Accommodations Industry: The Keys to Brand Love and Brand Loyalty for Hotels and Airbnb. *Journal of Travel Research*, 59(1), 173-189.

Behavioral experience
Definition: Behavioral experience with a brand is affiliated with the physical benefits that consumers receive from particular brand stimuli (e.g., physical actions or interactive experiences). The behavioral experience can be utilized as critical marketing practice because physical and interactive.

> Source: Kang, J., Kwun, D. J. & Hahm, J. J. (2020). Turning Your Customers into Brand Evangelists: Evidence from Cruise Travelers. *Journal of Quality Assurance in Hospitality & Tourism, 21*(6), 617-643.

Behavioral involvement

Definition: Behavioral involvement is often used as alternative measures for the identification of unobservable attitudinal involvement.

> Source: Kim, S., Kim, S. & Petrick, J. F. (2019). The Effect of Film Nostalgia on Involvement, Familiarity, and Behavioral Intentions. Journal of Travel Research, 58(2), 283-297.

Behavioral loyalty

Definition: Behavioral loyalty denotes customers' behavior to repurchase since they enjoy a particular brand or service.

> Source: Agyei, J., Sun, S., Abrokwah, E., Penney, E. K. & Ofori-Boafo, R. (2020). Influence of Trust on Customer Engagement: Empirical Evidence From the Insurance Industry in Ghana. SAGE Open, 10(1), 2158244019899104.

Benevolence

Definition (1): Benevolence is detected when the brand displays a deep commitment to the welfare of the community and society that it serves.

> Source: Portal, S., Abratt, R. & Bendixen, M. (2018). Building a human brand: Brand anthropomorphism unravelled. *Business Horizons, 61*(3), 367-374

Definition (2): Benevolence refers to consumers' beliefs on sellers' good intentions towards privileging consumers' interests in a situation of vulnerability.

> Source: Langaro, D., de Fátima Salgueiro, M., Rita, P. & Del Chiappa, G. (2019). Users' Participation in Facebook Brand Pages and Its Influence on Word-of-Mouth: The Role of Brand Knowledge and Brand Relationship. Journal of Creative Communications, 14(3), 177-195.

Brand

Definition (1): Brand refers to the set of expectations, memories, stories and relationships that, taken together, account for a consumer's decision to choose one product or service over another."

> Source: Story, J. (2020). Brands we love to hate: differences in perceived versus observed driver behaviors. Journal of Marketing Theory and Practice, 28(3), 242-255.

Definition (2): Brand is defined as a set of intangible assets with the ability to engage the customer to the firm is another form of value.

> Source: González-Mansilla, Ó., Berenguer-Contrí, G. & Serra-Cantallops, A. (2019). The impact of value co-creation on hotel brand equity and customer satisfaction. *Tourism Management, 75,* 51-65.

Definition (3): The signaling theory of brand marketing suggests that a brand can be regarded as a signal of the marketing mix of the seller and perceived quality of the product.

> **Source:** Zhang, C., Kashmiri, S. & Cinelli, M. (2019). How Does Brand Age Influence Consumer Attitudes Toward a Firm's Unethical Behavior? *Journal of Business Ethics, 158*(3), 699-711.

Definition (4): Brand is defined as a collection of perceptions held in the mind of a consumer and it is constituted by various components, including corporation name and image, corporate culture, and a logo.

> **Source:** Zhang, M., Li, L., Ye, Y., Qin, K. & Zhong, J. (2020). The effect of brand anthropomorphism, brand distinctiveness, and warmth on brand attitude: A mediated moderation model. *Journal of Consumer Behaviour, 19*(5), 523-536.

Definition (5): Brand is a distinctive name or symbol that adds value (emotional, experiential, and symbolic) over and above its functional performance.

> **Source:** Dean, D., Arroyo-Gamez, R. E., Punjaisri, K. & Pich, C. (2016). Internal brand co-creation: The experiential brand meaning cycle in higher education. *Journal of Business Research, 69*(8), 3041-3048.

Definition (6): Brand has been defined as a customer experience represented by a collection of images and ideas and often it refers to a symbol such as a name, logo, slogan, and design scheme.

> **Source:** Flight Richard, L. & Coker Kesha, K. (2016). Brand constellations: reflections of the emotional self. *Journal of Product & Brand Management, 25*(2), 134-147.

Definition (7): Brand is defined as a name, term, sign, symbol or design or combination that is intended to identify the products and services of a seller or group of sellers and differentiate them from competitors.

> **Source:** Wakefield, L. T. & Wakefield, R. L. (2018). Anxiety and Ephemeral Social Media Use in Negative eWOM Creation. *Journal of Interactive Marketing, 41*, 44-59.

Definition (8): A brand is defned as a cluster of values that enables a promise to be made about a unique and welcoming experience.

> **Source:** Brunetti, F., Confente, I. & Kaufmann, H. R. (2019). The human dimension of a brand influences brand equity: an empirical examination in the context of a luxury and a convenience brand. *Journal of Brand Management, 26*(6), 634-645.

Brand acquaintancing

Definition: An acquaintance brand is not a stranger who merits indifference, and not a friend who merits cognitive or emotional energy.

> **Source:** Sashittal, Hemant & Jassawalla, Avan. (2019). Preliminary evidence of brand acquaintancing on Snapchat. *Marketing Intelligence & Planning.* 37.

Brand activation

Definition: Brand activation is defined as the actual behavior of customers, which explicitly represented by the interactions of customers with brand and community.

> **Source:** Duong, G. H., Wu, W.-Y. & Le, L. H. (2020). The effects of brand page characteristics on customer brand engagement: moderating roles of community involvement and comedy production contents. *Journal of Brand Management*, 27(5), 531-545.

Brand addiction

Definition: Brand addiction is defined as a chronic, relapsing brain disease that is characterized by compulsive brand seeking and use, despite some harmful consequences.

> **Source:** Cui, C. C., Mrad, M. & Hogg, M. K. (2018). Brand addiction: Exploring the concept and its definition through an experiential lens. Journal of Business Research, 87, 118-127.

Brand admiration

Definition: Brand admiration is an important measure of consumer-brand relationship and established brand love, brand trust, and brand respect as the three key elements of brand admiration.

> **Source:** Trivedi, J. & Sama, R. (2020). The Effect of Influencer Marketing on Consumers' Brand Admiration and Online Purchase Intentions: An Emerging Market Perspective. Journal of Internet Commerce, 19(1), 103-124.

Brand advocacy

Definition: Brand advocacy refers to the protection of the brand by its consumers. There are three types of brand advocacy behaviors: positive word of mouth, resistance to negative information, and intention to invest in the company.

> **Source:** Kumar, V. & Kaushik, A. K. (2020). Does experience affect engagement? Role of destination brand engagement in developing brand advocacy and revisit intentions. *Journal of Travel & Tourism Marketing*, 37(3), 332-346.

Brand aesthetic

Definition: Brand aesthetic is a dimension of brand salience (i.e., brand aesthetic association and utilitarian attributes association).

> **Source:** Park, H. H., Jeon, J. O. & Sullivan, P. (2015). How does visual merchandising in fashion retail stores affect consumers' brand attitude and purchase intention? *The International Review of Retail, Distribution and Consumer Research*, 25(1), 87-104.

Brand afection

Definition: Brand afection is described as emotions, feelings, moods, and attitudes toward a brand.

> **Source:** Duong, G. H., Wu, W.-Y. & Le, L. H. (2020). The effects of brand page characteristics on customer brand engagement: moderating roles of community involvement and comedy production contents. *Journal of Brand Management, 27*(5), 531-545.

Brand affect

Definition (1): Brand affect refers to consumers' emotional feelings about an object or event, or whether they like or dislike a brand and it is an important element to customer–brand relationship which is based on customers' feelings. Brand affect refers to a consumer's affective feelings about a particular brand.

> **Source:** Chen-Yu, J., Cho, S. & Kincade, D. (2016). Brand perception and brand repurchase intent in online apparel shopping: An examination of brand experience, image congruence, brand affect, and brand trust. *Journal of Global Fashion Marketing, 7*(1), 30-44

Brand affiliation

Definition: Brand affiliation, could be defined as the motivation of the consumer to follow a brand on social media due to the fact that the brand is convergent with the consumer's lifestyle, possession desires and preferences.

> **Source:** Bento, M., Martinez, L. M. & Martinez, L. F. (2018). Brand engagement and search for brands on social media: Comparing Generations X and Y in Portugal. *Journal of Retailing and Consumer Services, 43*, 234-241.

Brand affinity

Definition: Brand affinity is defined as a feeling of liking, sympathy, or attachment toward a specific brand.

> **Source:** Siew, S.-W., Minor, M. S. & Felix, R. (2018). The influence of perceived strength of brand origin on willingness to pay more for luxury goods. *Journal of Brand Management, 25*(6), 591-605.

Brand age

Definition: Brand age reflects the length of time that a brand has existed which reflects a brand's longevity in the competitive marketplace. The brand age is an important extrinsic cue that can positively influence consumers' evaluations.

> **Source:** Zhang, C., Kashmiri, S. & Cinelli, M. (2019). How Does Brand Age Influence Consumer Attitudes Toward a Firm's Unethical Behavior? *Journal of Business Ethics, 158*(3), 699-711.

Brand alignment

Definition: Brand alignment is defined as the extent to which the brand featured in the store is perceived as congruent with other brands sold by the retailer.

> **Source:** Badrinarayanan, V. & Becerra, E. P. (2019). Antecedents and consequences of shoppers' attitude toward branded store-within-stores: An exploratory framework. *Journal of Business Research, 105*, 189-200.

Brand alliance

Definition: Brand alliance refers to adding a brand to a product offering that includes brands from another company.

> **Source:** Voss, K. E. & Mohan, M. (2016). Corporate brand effects in brand alliances. *Journal of Business Research, 69*(10), 4177-4184.

Brand ambassador

Definition: Brand ambassor appears as a synonym as brand evangelist (*see Brand Evangelist*).

> **Source:** Schmidt, H. J. & Baumgarth, C. (2018). Strengthening internal brand equity with brand ambassador programs: development and testing of a success factor model. *Journal of Brand Management, 25*(3), 250-265.

Brand ambassador program

Definition: Brand ambassador program is characterized by goal-oriented (increasing internal brand equity, through brand knowledge, brand commitment and brand behaviour of employees) and planned

> **Source:** Schmidt, H. J. & Baumgarth, C. (2018). Strengthening internal brand equity with brand ambassador programs: development and testing of a success factor model. *Journal of Brand Management, 25*(3), 250-265.

Brand anthropomorphism

Definition (1): Anthropomorphism describes the tendency to imbue nonhuman agents with human characteristics, motivations, intentions, and emotions.

> **Source:** Zhang, M., Li, L., Ye, Y., Qin, K. & Zhong, J. (2020). The effect of brand anthropomorphism, brand distinctiveness, and warmth on brand attitude: A mediated moderation model. *Journal of Consumer Behaviour, 19*(5), 523-536.

Definition (2): Brand anthropomorphism refers to a brand positioning strategy of using humanlike visual and verbal elements to enhance consumer attributions of human characteristics to a brand.

> **Source:** Kwak, H., Puzakova, M. & Rocereto, J. F. (2017). When brand anthropomorphism alters perceptions of justice: The moderating role of self-construal. *International Journal of Research in Marketing, 34*(4), 851-871.

Definition (3): Brand anthropomorphism is defined as perception by consumers as actual human beings with various emotional states, minds, souls, and conscious behaviors that may act as important factors in social ties.

> Source: Zhang, M., Li, L., Ye, Y., Qin, K. & Zhong, J. (2020). The effect of brand anthropomorphism, brand distinctiveness, and warmth on brand attitude: Amediated moderation model. Journal of Consumer Behaviour, 19(5), 523-536.

Definition (4): Brand anthropomorphism refers to consumers' tendency to attribute human-like features such as intentions, emotions, motivations, and mind to brands.

> Source: Bernritter, S. F., Verlegh, P. W. J. & Smit, E. G. (2016). Why Nonprofits Are Easier to Endorse on Social Media: The Roles of Warmth and Brand Symbolism. Journal of Interactive Marketing, 33, 27-42.

Brand anthropomorphization

Definition: Brand anthropomorphization refers to a process of brand anthropomorphism.

> Source: Zhang, M., Li, L., Ye, Y., Qin, K. & Zhong, J. (2020). The effect of brand anthropomorphism, brand distinctiveness, and warmth on brand attitude: Amediated moderation model. Journal of Consumer Behaviour, 19(5), 523-536.

Brand app resistance

Definition: Brand app resistance is characterized as users resist to a brand app provided by the organization owning the brand through the act of adopting other service channels.

> Source: Cheng, Y.-Y., Tung, W.-F., Yang, M.-H. & Chiang, C.-T. (2019). Linking relationship equity to brand resonance in a social networking brand community. Electronic Commerce Research and Applications, 35, 100849.

Brand appeal

Definition: Brand appeal is defined as an attractive, productive, and special brand.

> Source: Rauschnabel, P. A., Krey, N., Babin, B. J. & Ivens, B. S. (2016). Brand management in higher education: The University Brand Personality Scale. Journal of Business Research, 69(8), 3077-3086.

Brand architecture

Definition (1): Brand architecture is defined as a coherent structure organizing associated entities in hierarchical systems representing the relationships between different brands

> Source: Åsberg, P. & Uggla, H. (2019). Apresentando a arquitetura de marca multidimensional: levando em consideração a estrutura, a orientação para o mercado

Brand associations

Definition (1): Brand associations are defined as the informational nodes linked to the brand node in memory and contain the meaning of the brand for consumers.

>Source: Baumann, C., Hamin, H. & Chong, A. (2015). The role of brand exposure and experience on brand recall—Product durables vis-à-vis FMCG. *Journal of Retailing and Consumer Services*, 23, 21-31.

Definition (2): Brand association is defined as the image dimensions that are unique to a
brand, and it can create value for the brand and its customers by helping to process/retrieve information, differentiate the brand and create positive attitudes.

>Source: Zhang, J., Jiang, Y., Shabbir, R. & Zhu, M. (2016). How brand orientation impacts B2B service brand equity? An empirical study among Chinese firms. *Journal of Business & Industrial Marketing*, 31(1), 83-98.

Definition (3): Brand associations are the informational nodes encompassing knowledge pertaining to the different facets of a brand.

>Source: Mann, B. J. S., Parmar, Y. & Ghuman, M. K. (2020) A New Scale to Capture the Multidimensionality of Celebrity Image. *Global Business Review*, 0(0), 0972150920919599

Definition (4): Brand associations is a mental representation of a brand and are defined as those associations that are unique to the brand and differentiate the brand from other brands in a category.

>Source: Jeon Jung, O. & Baeck, S. (2016). What drives consumer's responses to brand crisis? The moderating roles of brand associations and brand-customer relationship strength. *Journal of Product & Brand Management*, 25(6), 550-567.

Definition (5): Brand association refers to everything related to the brand in consumers' minds and can help consumers figure out the relevance of the parent brand and the extended brand.

>Source: Ahn, J., Park, J. K. & Hyun, H. (2018). Luxury product to service brand extension and brand equity transfer. *Journal of Retailing and Consumer Services*, 42, 22-28.

Brand atributes

Definition: Brand atributes are the characteristics of the brand that should be original, ethical, genuine, warmth, competence, and trust.

> Source: Portal, S., Abratt, R. & Bendixen, M. (2018). Building a human brand: Brand anthropomorphism unravelled. *Business Horizons*, *61*(3), 367-374.

Brand attachment

Definition (1): According to attachment theory, consumers tend to establish strong emotional affiliations with a brand through brand personification where brand attachment is defined as the strength of the cognitive and affective bond between a brand and the consumer self.

> Source: Kang, J., Kwun, D. J. & Hahm, J. J. (2020). Turning Your Customers into Brand Evangelists: Evidence from Cruise Travelers. *Journal of Quality Assurance in Hospitality & Tourism*, *21*(6), 617-643.

Definition (2): A consumer is attached to a brand if he/she perceives it as a source of symbolic gratification or a way to enhance or reinforce his/her self-concept. In this context, the brand attachment includes the psychological benefits associated with a brand in the consumer mind.

> Source: Korai, B. (2017). Determinants of African Women's Brand Sensitivity Toward Cosmetics. *Journal of International Consumer Marketing*, *29*(4), 250-264.

Definition (3): Brand attachment is the psychological bond between consumers and brand in which both parties are willing to allocate resources to maintain the relationship between them.

> Source: Pourazad, N., Stocchi, L. & Pare, V. (2019). Brand attribute associations, emotional consumer-brand relationship and evaluation of brand extensions. *Australasian Marketing Journal (AMJ)*, *27*(4), 249-260.

Definition (4): Brand attachment is a psychological construct which refers to the internal connection of the consumer to the brand

> Source: Koronaki, E., Kyrousi, A. G. & Panigyrakis, G. G. (2018). The emotional value of arts-based initiatives: Strengthening the luxury brand–consumer relationship. *Journal of Business Research*, *85*, 406-413.

Definition (5): Brand attachment, as the strength of the bond connecting the brand with the self, comprises three principal dimensions, including self-connection, emotions, and importance.

> Source: Roy, V., Tata, S. V. & Parsad, C. (2018). Consumer response to brand involved in food safety scandal: An exploratory study based on a recent scandal in India. *Journal of Consumer Behaviour*, *17*(1), 25-33.

Brand attack

Definition: Brand attack occurs when the brand is hijacked for a destructively negative re-imagining of its meanings.

> Source: Kristal, S., Baumgarth, C. & Henseler, J. (2018). Brand play versus Brand attack: the subversion of brand meaning in non-collaborative co-creation by professional artists and consumer activists. *Journal of Product & Brand Management*, *27*, 334-347.

Brand attitude

Definition: Brand attitude can be defined as consumer's overall evaluation of a brand around favorable or unfavorable responses to brand-related stimuli or conviction.

>**Source:** Kudeshia, C. & Kumar, A. (2017). Social eWOM: does it affect the brand attitude and purchase intention of brands? *Management Research Review*, *40*(3), 310-330.

Brand attitude change

Definition: Brand attitude change refers to the evolution of consumer attitude toward the newly created brand system as compared with the master brand.

>**Source:** Azar Salim, L., Aimé, I. & Ulrich, I. (2018). Brand gender-bending: The impact of an endorsed brand strategy on consumers' evaluation of gendered mixed-target brands. *European Journal of Marketing*, *52*(7/8), 1598-1624.

Brand attractiveness

Definition: Brand attractiveness refers to the positive evaluation of the brand's central, distinctive, and enduring associations and characteristics.

>**Source:** Elbedweihy, A. M., Jayawardhena, C., Elsharnouby, M. H. & Elsharnouby, T. H. (2016). Customer relationship building: The role of brand attractiveness and consumer–brand identification. *Journal of Business Research*, *69*(8), 2901-2910.

Brand attribute association

Definition: Brand attribute associations can be defined as descriptive features that help characterise a brand such as the image the consumer associate with a given brand, the intangible benefits it offers, and the factors involved in the process of purchasing.

>**Source:** Pourazad, N., Stocchi, L. & Pare, V. (2019). Brand attribute associations, emotional consumer-brand relationship and evaluation of brand extensions. *Australasian Marketing Journal (AMJ)*, *27*(4), 249-260.

Brand aura

Definition: Brand aura can be defined as an eradiation of the spiritual and charismatic values of a particular brand which is a predictor of the high consumers' trust in the brand and brand attachment.

>**Source:** Wahyuni, S. & Fitriani, N. (2017). Brand religiosity aura and brand loyalty in Indonesia Islamic banking. *Journal of Islamic Marketing*, *8*(3), 361-372.

Brand authenticity

Definition (1): Brand authenticity is a multifaceted construct that contains various ontological assumptions, perspectives, and typologies. At the most basic level, brand authenticity can be defined as genuine.

> **Source:** Mody, M. & Hanks, L. (2020). Consumption Authenticity in the Accommodations Industry: The Keys to Brand Love and Brand Loyalty for Hotels and Airbnb. *Journal of Travel Research, 59*(1), 173-189.

Definition (2): Brand authenticity is mainly related to the preservation of cultural norms, beliefs and values throughout the brand.

> **Source:** Fritz, K., Schoenmueller, V. & Bruhn, M. (2017). Authenticity in branding – exploring antecedents and consequences of brand authenticity. *European Journal of Marketing, 51*(2), 324-348.

Definition (3): Brand authenticity is defined as the extent to which consumers perceive that a brand's managers are intrinsically motivated in that they are passionate about and devoted to providing their products.

> **Source:** Moulard, J. G., Raggio, R. D. & Folse, J. A. G. (2016). Brand Authenticity: Testing the Antecedents and Outcomes of Brand Management's Passion for its Products. *Psychology & Marketing, 33*(6), 421-436.

Definition (4): Brand authenticity is defined as the extent to which consumers perceive a brand to be faithful toward itself, true to its consumers (credibility), motivated by caring and responsibility (integrity), and able to support consumers in being true.

> **Source:** Roy, V., Tata, S. V. & Parsad, C. (2018). Consumer response to brand involved in food safety scandal: An exploratory study based on a recent scandal in India. *Journal of Consumer Behaviour, 17*(1), 25-33.

Definition (5): Brand authenticity differs from corporate reputation in fundamental ways: first, brand authenticity is a brand image component which describes the position of a brand in the market in terms of how consumers see it.

> **Source:** Guèvremont, A. & Grohmann, B. (2018). Does brand authenticity alleviate the effect of brand scandals? *Journal of Brand Management, 25*(4), 322-336

Definition (6): Brand authenticity is a judgment that observable characteristics or actions associated with the brand are consistent with the brand's identity and true self.

> **Source:** Hamby, A., Brinberg, D. & Daniloski, K. (2019). It's about our values: How founder's stories influence brand authenticity. *Psychology & Marketing, 36*(11), 1014-1026

Definition (7): Brand authenticity is a brand's genuineness, uniqueness, ability to keep its promises and unaffectedness as perceived by consumers through both brand behavior and brand image.

> **Source:** Jian, Y., Zhou, Z. & Zhou, N. (2019). Brand cultural symbolism, brand authenticity, and consumer well-being: the moderating role of cultural involvement. *Journal of Product & Brand Management, 28*(4), 529-539.

Brand avoidance

Definition: Brand avoidance is defined as the phenomenon whereby consumers deliberately choose to keep away from or reject a brand. Brand avoidance as a concept is only applicable when consumers avoid brands even though they are available.

> **Source:** Knittel, Z., Beurer, K. & Berndt, A. (2016). Brand avoidance among Generation Y consumers. *Qualitative Market Research: An International Journal*, 19(1), 27-43.

Brand awareness

Definition (1): Brand awareness refers to a consumer's brand recall or brand recognition that has a positive effect on consumer decision making and brand image.

> **Source:** Molinillo, S., Japutra, A., Nguyen, B. & Chen Cheng-Hao, S. (2017). Responsible brands vs active brands? An examination of brand personality on brand awareness, brand trust, and brand loyalty. Marketing Intelligence & Planning, 35(2), 166-179.

Definition (2): Brand awareness represents the ability of customers to recall a brand name (brand recall) and capability of customers to identify a brand in the presence of a brand cue (brand recognition).

> **Source:** Dabbous, A. & Barakat, K. A. (2020). Bridging the online offline gap: Assessing the impact of brands' social network content quality on brand awareness and purchase intention. *Journal of Retailing and Consumer Services*, 53, 101966.

Definition (3): Brand awareness refers to the strength of a brand's presence in consumers' minds and defines the ability for a buyer to recognize or recall that a brand is a member of a certain product category. The brand awareness dimensions are brand recognition, brand recall, brand familiarity, top-of-mind awareness, recall of advertising, brand dominance.

> **Source:** Foroudi, P. (2019). Influence of brand signature, brand awareness, brand attitude, brand reputation on hotel industry's brand performance. *International Journal of Hospitality Management*, 76, 271-285.

Definition (4): Brand awareness is a first dimension of brand knowledge. It refers to the strength of the brand node in memory (i.e., how easy it is for the consumer to remember the brand).

> **Source:** Barreda, A. A., Bilgihan, A., Nusair, K. & Okumus, F. (2016). Online branding: Development of hotel branding through interactivity theory. *Tourism Management*, 57, 180-192.

Brand belief

Definition: Brand beliefs can be functional, experiential, and symbolic and represent the personal value and meanings that consumers attach to the brand. and can be functional, experiential, and symbolic.

Source: Micu, C. C., Sciandra, M. R. & Micu, A. (2019). Understanding Social Media: The Effect of Belief Type and Product Type on Consumers' Social Media Use. *Journal of Marketing Theory and Practice*, 27(1), 55-66.

Brand benefits

Definition (1): Brand benefits represent the added value of the brand image to the customer. Brand benefits are commonly stressed in positioning strategies (quality, uniqueness, leading position, and growing popularity) in determining brand purchase intentions.

Source: Krautz, C. (2017). A Cross-Cultural Study of Collective Brand Perceptions Within The Brand Equity Framework. *Journal of Marketing Theory and Practice*, 25(3), 274-290.

Brand benevolence

Definition: Brand benevolence is a cognitive type of reputation which is based on the functional capability of a brand. Brand benevolence is defined as a sincere concern for customers' interests and the motivation to do good for them.

Source: Foroudi, P. (2019). Influence of brand signature, brand awareness, brand attitude, brand reputation on hotel industry's brand performance. *International Journal of Hospitality Management*, 76, 271-285.

Brand biographies

Definition: Brand biographies are brand stories that focus on the brand's origin and growth
over time. The ingredients of brand biography include the concepts of product design, the origin of brand and the memorial stories during the initial stage .

Source: Nguyen, T.-T. & Grohmann, B. (2020). The influence of passion/determination and external disadvantage on consumer responses to brand biographies. *Journal of Brand Management*, 27(4), 452-465.

Brand building behavior

Definition: Brand building behavior concept may be involved in brand building by both internal marketing (e.g., employee training, organization culture orientation, and management styles) and external marketing (e.g., advertising).

Source: Xie, L., Li, Y., Chen, S.-H. & Huan, T.-C. (2016). Triad theory of hotel managerial leadership, employee brand-building behavior, and guest images of luxury-hotel brands. *International Journal of Contemporary Hospitality Management*, 28(9), 1826-1847.

Brand centred control

Definition: Brand-centred control as a new form of normative control which is the attempt to bring out and direct the required efforts of members by controlling the experiences, thoughts, and feelings that guide their actions.

Source: Müller, M. (2017). 'Brand-Centred Control': A Study of Internal Branding and Normative Control. *Organization Studies*, *38*(7), 895-915.)

Brand champion
Definition: Brand champion can be defined as committed individuals who are willing to evangelise on behalf of a brand.

Source: Yakimova, R., Mavondo, F., Freeman, S. & Stuart, H. (2017). Brand champion behaviour: Its role in corporate branding. *Journal of Brand Management*, *24*(6), 575-591.

Brand character
Definition: Brand character is defined as a brand mascot

Source: Angle, J. W., Dagogo-Jack, S. W., Forehand, M. R. & Perkins, A. W. (2017). Activating stereotypes with brand imagery: The role of viewer political identity. *Journal of Consumer Psychology*, *27*(1), 84-90.

Brand characteristic
Definition: Brand characteristic is defined as intrinsic and extrinsic attributes (product design, material used and logo design) can also influence a consumer's evaluation process.

Source: Azar Salim, L., Aimé, I. & Ulrich, I. (2018). Brand gender-bending: The impact of an endorsed brand strategy on consumers' evaluation of gendered mixed-target brands. *European Journal of Marketing*, *52*(7/8), 1598-1624.

Brand charisma
Definition: Brand charisma is defined as a concept that is socially constructed by associating the brand with an emotional metaphor of something transcendent or sacred, thus allowing their owners to engage in a hoped-for dream of high-status.

Source: Semaan, R. W., Ashill, N. & Williams, P. (2019). Sophisticated, iconic and magical: A qualitative analysis of brand charisma. *Journal of Retailing and Consumer Services*, *49*, 102-113.

Brand choice attainment
Definition: Brand choice attainment is the process why consumers choose specific brands
and the mechanisms through which brand choice decisions are made.

Source: Elsharnouby Tamer, H. (2016). Participation behaviour among international students: The role of satisfaction with service augmentation and brand choice attainment. *International Journal of Educational Management*, *30*(5), 679-697.

Brand citizenship behavior

Definition (1): Brand citizenship behavior refers to a voluntary behavior that helps benefit a brand (e.g. brand enthusiasm, brand endorsement and helping behavior).

> **Source:** Kim, S.-H., Kim, M. & Lee, S. (2019). The consumer value-based brand citizenship behavior model: Evidence from local and global coffee businesses. *Journal of Hospitality Marketing & Management, 28*(4), 472-490.

Definition (2): Brand citizenship behaviour is defined as proactive behaviors on the part of a salesperson that is outside the scope of the job description but that contribute to the viability and vitality of the brand.

> **Source** Nyadzayo, M. W., Matanda, M. J. & Ewing, M. T. (2016). Franchisee-based brand equity: The role of brand relationship quality and brand citizenship behavior. *Industrial Marketing Management, 52*, 163-174.

Definition (3): Brand citizenship behaviour refers to employee behaviour that is consistent with the overarching values and identity of the brand and the brand promise, which strengthens the brand.

> **Source:** Karanges, E., Johnston, K. A., Lings, I. & Beatson, A. T. (2018). Brand signalling: An antecedent of employee brand understanding. *Journal of Brand Management, 25*(3), 235-249.

Brand clarity

Definition: Brand clarity depicts the communicated comprehensibility of the brand's communication style.

> **Source:** Fritz, K., Schoenmueller, V. & Bruhn, M. (2017). Authenticity in branding – exploring antecedents and consequences of brand authenticity. *European Journal of Marketing, 51*(2), 324-348.

Brand co-creation

Definition: Brand co-creation could be seen as the marketers integrate firm competencies with consumer participation to enhance the value of brand.

> **Source:** Hsieh, S. H. & Chang, A. (2016). The Psychological Mechanism of Brand Co-creation Engagement. *Journal of Interactive Marketing, 33*, 13-26.

Brand co-creation engagement

Definition: Brand co-creation engagement is a persistent, positive affective-motivational state of fulfilment that is characterized by vigour, dedication, and absorption during brand co-creation.

> **Source:** Hsieh, S. H. & Chang, A. (2016). The Psychological Mechanism of Brand Co-creation Engagement. *Journal of Interactive Marketing, 33*, 13-26.

Brand code

Definition: Brand code can be defined as a complex, emergent mental structure, arising from brand experiences, representing that what the brand stands for: its brand meaning.

> **Source:** Stach, J. (2019). Meaningful experiences: an embodied cognition perspective on brand meaning co-creation. *Journal of Brand Management, 26*(3), 317-331.

Brand commitment

Definition (1): Brand commitment is based on interpersonal relationship theory and is generally defined as the extent of psychological attachment that individuals feel toward the brand. Brand commitment is conceptualized either as a one-dimensional or a two-dimensional concept split into affective commitment (based on loyalty and a feeling of belonging) and continuance commitment (based on rational evaluation).

> **Source:** Giovanis, A. N. & Athanasopoulou, P. (2018). Consumer-brand relationships and brand loyalty in technology-mediated services. *Journal of Retailing and Consumer Services, 40,* 287-294.

Definition (2): Brand commitment is defined as an enduring desire and willingness to maintaining a brand relationship and represents the extent to which stakeholders are willing to work for the brand and its success.

> **Source:** Merz, M. A., Zarantonello, L. & Grappi, S. (2018). How valuable are your customers in the brand value co-creation process? The development of a Customer Co-Creation Value (CCCV) scale. *Journal of Business Research, 82,* 79-89.

Brand communication

Definition: Brand communication is the language, the media, the style that a brand sends their mensages (e.g., figurative language, assertive language, or language that implies closeness) in an advertising context affect consumer behavior.

> **Source:** Gretry, A., Horváth, C., Belei, N. & van Riel, A. C. R. (2017). "Don't pretend to be my friend!" When an informal brand communication style backfires on social media. *Journal of Business Research, 74,* 77-89.

Brand community

Definition (1): Brand community is defined as a group which are built around a specific brand.

> **Source:** Popp, B. & Woratschek, H. (2016). Introducing branded communities in sport for building strong brand relations in social media. *Sport Management Review, 19*(2), 183-197.

Definition (2): Brand community identity is the shared social identity at the group level internalized by individual members who depersonalize their individual identity.

> Source: Black, I. & Veloutsou, C. (2017). Working consumers: Co-creation of brand identity, consumer identity and brand community identity. *Journal of Business Research, 70*, 416-429.

Definition (3): Brand community is described as a specialized, nongeographically bound community, based on a structured set of social relationships among admirers of a brand

> Source: Kumar, J. & Nayak Jogendra, K. (2019). Brand engagement without brand ownership: a case of non-brand owner community members. *Journal of Product & Brand Management, 28*(2), 216-230.

Definition (4): Brand community is a group wich is based on a structured set of social relations among admirers of a brand and is inherently equipped with the attributes of rituals, traditions, a shared consciousness between individuals.

> Source: Cheng, Y.-Y., Tung, W.-F., Yang, M.-H. & Chiang, C.-T. (2019). Linking relationship equity to brand resonance in a social networking brand community. *Electronic Commerce Research and Applications, 35*, 100849.

Brand community identification

Definition (1): Brand community identification is defined how the person construes himself or herself to be a member (as 'belonging') to the brand community and arises if a member perceives similarity between his or her self-identity and identities of brand community.

> Source: Mandl, L. & Hogreve, J. (2020). Buffering effects of brand community identification in service failures: The role of customer citizenship behaviors. *Journal of Business Research, 107*, 130-137.

Definition (2): Brand community identification signals the strength of consumer connection with the brand community and represents the individual construes himself or herself to be a member to the brand community.

> Source Chang, A., Hsieh Sara, H. & Tseng Timmy, H. (2013). Online brand community response to negative brand events: the role of group eWOM. *Internet Research, 23*(4), 486-506.

Brand compass

Definition: Brand compass is viewed as a firm asset or resource that underpins organisational capabilities and performance.

> Source: Bridson, K. C. & Evans, J. (2018). Brand compass: charting a course to improve firm performance. *Journal of Strategic Marketing, 26*(2), 174-187.

Brand compatibility

Definition: Brand compatibility is defined as the extent to which you prefer, in accordance with the same similar brand preference.

Source: Charlton, A. B. & Cornwell, T. B. (2019). Authenticity in horizontal marketing partnerships: A better measure of brand compatibility. *Journal of Business Research*, 100, 279-298.

Brand competence

Definition: Brand competence is a brand's ability to achieve its goals.

Source: Wang, H. & Liu, D. (2020). The differentiated impact of perceived brand competence type on brand extension evaluation. *Journal of Business Research*, 117, 400-410.

Brand competitiveness

Definition: Brand competitiveness reflects upon the ability of the brand to drive the market better than competitors in a marketplace.

Source: Gupta, S., Gallear, D., Rudd, J. & Foroudi, P. (2020). The impact of brand value on brand competitiveness. *Journal of Business Research*, 112, 210-222.

Brand concept

Definition: Brand concept is the unique and abstract meanings associated with brands. Similar to human value, brand concept reflects the ultimate goal the brand pursues.

Source: Zhu, H., Li, Q. & Liao, J. (2018). Doing well when doing good: the fit between corporate sponsorship and brand concept. *Journal of Consumer Marketing*, 35(7), 733-742.

Brand connection

Definition: Brand connection is defined as the links that consumers create between a brand and their own identity. Brands are perceived to be more important to a consumer the more closely the brands are linked to the self.

Source: Harrigan, P., Evers, U., Miles, M. P. & Daly, T. (2018). Customer engagement and the relationship between involvement, engagement, self-brand connection and brand usage intent. *Journal of Business Research*, 88, 388-396.

Brand consciousness

Definition (1): Brand consciousness is a consumer's mental orientation in choosing well-known brand-name products. Brand consciousness of consumers refers to believing that the brand image and strong brand names stand for good quality, and their willingness to pay.

Source: Yang, K., Kim, J. & Kim, Y.-K. (2017). The effect of brand consciousness on interpersonal influences, brand values, and purchase intention: Cases for American and Korean college students. *Journal of Global Fashion Marketing*, 8(2), 83-97.

Definition (2): Brand consciousness is defined as the psychological preference towards famous brand name goods and is a tendency to buy expensive and famous brands, believing that higher price reflects higher quality.

Source: Sharda, N. & Bhat, A. (2019). Role of consumer vanity and the mediating effect of brand consciousness in luxury consumption. *Journal of Product & Brand Management, 28*(7), 800-811.

Brand consistency

Definition: Brand consistency denotes the similarity in associations between the brand extension and the brand concept and measures how similar a product's aesthetic design is to the average aesthetics of its brand.

Source: Liu, Y., Li, K. J., Chen, H. & Balachander, S. (2017). The Effects of Products' Aesthetic Design on Demand and Marketing-Mix Effectiveness: The Role of Segment Prototypicality and Brand Consistency. *Journal of Marketing, 81*(1), 83-102.

Brand constellation

Definition: Brand (or product) constellation refers to clusters of complementary products, specific brands, and/or consumption activities used by consumers to define, communicate and enact social roles.

Source: Flight Richard, L. & Coker Kesha, K. (2016). Brand constellations: reflections of the emotional self. *Journal of Product & Brand Management, 25*(2), 134-147

Brand coolness

Definition: Brand coolness is a multidimensional construct that encompasses high status, aesthetically appealing, original and energy.

Source: Warren, C., Batra, R., Loureiro, S. M. C. & Bagozzi, R. P. (2019). Brand Coolness. *Journal of Marketing, 83*(5), 36-56.

Brand creativity

Definition: Brand creativity is related to the extent to which the stakeholder is stimulated by the brand in terms of his/her use of imagination and the development of original ideas. Brand creativity represents customers' production, conceptualization, or development of novel and useful ideas and process.

Source: Merz, M. A., Zarantonello, L. & Grappi, S. (2018). How valuable are your customers in the brand value co-creation process? The development of a Customer Co-Creation Value (CCCV) scale. *Journal of Business Research, 82*, 79-89.

Brand credibility

Definition (1): Brand credibility is the ability and willingness of brands to deliver on their promises and is defined as the believability of the product information contained in a brand.

> Source: Mandler, T., Bartsch, F. & Han, C. M. (2020). Brand credibility and marketplace globalization: The role of perceived brand globalness and localness. *Journal of International Business Studies*.

Definition (2): Brand credibility is a signal to be the believability of the product position information contained in a brand depends on a brand's ability and willingness to offer what it promises to customers.

> Source: Vuong, B. N. & Khanh Giao, H. N. (2020). The Impact of Perceived Brand Globalness on Consumers' Purchase Intention and the Moderating Role of Consumer Ethnocentrism: An Evidence from Vietnam. *Journal of International Consumer Marketing*, 32(1), 47-68.

Definition (3): Brand credibility refers to the degree to which consumers can believe in the validity of the product information presented by a brand, and requires that consumers view the brand as having the ability (i.e., competence) and willingness (i.e., trustworthiness).

> Source: Zhang, C., Kashmiri, S. & Cinelli, M. (2019). How Does Brand Age Influence Consumer Attitudes Toward a Firm's Unethical Behavior? *Journal of Business Ethics*, 158(3), 699-711.

Definition (4): Brand credibility of a brand is the believability of the information and promises that are attached to the brand and contains expertise and trustworthiness dimensions.

> Source: Zhang, B., Ritchie, B., Mair, J. & Driml, S. (2019). Is the Airline Trustworthy? The Impact of Source Credibility on Voluntary Carbon Offsetting. *Journal of Travel Research*, 58(5), 715-731.

Brand crisis

Definition (1): Brand crises are the negative incidents that threaten the reputations of the brand.

> Source: Roy, V., Tata, S. V. & Parsad, C. (2018). Consumer response to brand involved in food safety scandal: An exploratory study based on a recent scandal in India. *Journal of Consumer Behaviour*, 17(1), 25-33.

Definition (2): Brand crisis can result from true negative stories surfacing in the public sphere or can result from false rumours about the brand.

Source: Nadeau, J., Rutter, R. & Lettice, F. (2020). Social media responses and brand personality in product and moral harm crises: why waste a good crisis? *Journal of Marketing Management, 36*(11-12), 1031-1054.

Definition (3): A brand crisis occurs when a key brand proposition is unsubstantiated or false, a product is cited for failing to meet a mandatory safety standard, or a product defect is discovered that could cause substantial harm or unreasonable brand risk.

Source: Zou, P. & Li, G. (2016). How emerging market investors' value competitors' customer equity: Brand crisis spillover in China. *Journal of Business Research, 69*(9), 3765-3771.

Brand culture

Definition: Brand Culture can be defined as the DNA of the brand and its values.

Source: Carah, N. & Brodmerkel, S. (2020). Critical perspectives on brand culture in the era of participatory and algorithmic media. *Sociology Compass, 14*(2), e12752.

Brand cultural symbolism

Definition: Brand Cultural symbolism happens when customers adore the brand like a cultural symbol.

Source: Jian, Y., Zhou, Z. & Zhou, N. (2019). Brand cultural symbolism, brand authenticity, and consumer well-being: the moderating role of cultural involvement. *Journal of Product & Brand Management, 28*(4), 529-539.

Brand deletion

Definition: Brand deletion is associated with excluding brands in brand architecture and it often occurs when brands have problems in market acceptance and profitability.

Source: Shah, P. (2017). Culling the brand portfolio: brand deletion outcomes and success factors. *Management Research Review, 40*(4), 370-377.

Brand differentiation

Definition (1): Brand differentiation is a marketing process that shows the differences among different brand products. Using differentiation, the manufacturer tries to make a product more attractive to the end customer by contrasting its unique qualities with other competing products.

Source: Giri, B. C., Roy, B. & Maiti, T. (2017). Multi-manufacturer pricing and quality management strategies in the presence of brand differentiation and return policy. *Computers & Industrial Engineering, 105*, 146-157.

Definition (2): Brand differentiation is viewed as the process of adding a set of meaningful and valued differences to distinguish the company's offering from competitors' offerings.

> **Source:** Lopez, C. & Leenders, M. A. A. M. (2019). Building a local identity through sellout crowds: the impact of brand popularity, brand similarity, and brand diversity of music festivals. *Journal of Strategic Marketing*, 27(5), 435-450.

Brand dilution

Definition: Brand dilution occurs when as changes in brand equity due to market occurrences is negative (i.e., diluted brand equity).

> **Source:** Shin, H., Eastman, J. K. & Mothersbaugh, D. (2017). The effect of a limited-edition offer following brand dilution on consumer attitudes toward a luxury brand. *Journal of Retailing and Consumer Services*, 38, 59-70.

Brand dis-identification

Definition: Brand dis-identification is defined as a self-perception based on a cognitive separation between a person's identity and his/her perception of the identity of a brand.

> **Source:** Wong, T. C., Haddoud Mohamed, Y., Kwok, Y. K. & He, H. (2018). Examining the key determinants towards online pro-brand and anti-brand community citizenship behaviours: A two-stage approach. *Industrial Management & Data Systems*, 118(4), 850-872.

Brand distinctiveness

Definition: Brand distinctiveness refers to consumers' perceptions that the brand is unique from competitors and are able to develop a higher level of brand awareness and greater brand differentiation in their minds.

> **Source:** Kang, J., Kwun, D. J. & Hahm, J. J. (2020). Turning Your Customers into Brand Evangelists: Evidence from Cruise Travelers. *Journal of Quality Assurance in Hospitality & Tourism*, 21(6), 617-643.

Brand effect

Definition: Brand effect refers to the strength of a brand constituted through customer innovation perception that influences consumers to form brand preference and recommend the brand to others.

> **Source:** (Zameer, H., Wang, Y. & Yasmeen, H. (2019). Transformation of firm innovation activities into brand effect. *Marketing Intelligence & Planning*, 37(2), 226-240.

Brand elegance

Definition: Brand elegance is a dimension of brand luxury and encompasses a brand like exquisite and good taste.

> Source: Roux, E., Tafani, E. & Vigneron, F. (2017). Values associated with luxury brand consumption and the role of gender. *Journal of Business Research*, 71, 102-113.

Brand elements

Definition (1): Brand elements are primarily used as identifiers, which include elements such as brand name, URLs, logos, symbols, characters, spokespeople, slogans, jingles, packages, and signagebrand element, such as a logo.

> Source: Chen, H.-L. & Mathews, S. (2017). Experiential Brand Deployment: Improving Tourism Brand Evaluations. *Journal of Hospitality & Tourism Research*, 41(5), 539-559.

Definition (2): Brand elements (also referred to as identities) represent the verbal and visual information that identify and differentiate a product or brand These brand elements encompasses names, logos, symbols, colours, characters, packaging, and slogans.

> Source: Odoom, R. (2016). Brand marketing programs and consumer loyalty – evidence from mobile phone users in an emerging market. *Journal of Product & Brand Management*, 25(7), 651-662.

Brand embarrassment

Definition: Brand embarrassment refers to consumer's feeling of awkwardness based on the perception of getting negatively evaluated by others while consuming a brand in a social context.

> Source: Sarkar, A., Sarkar, J. G., Sreejesh, S., Anusree, M. R. & Rishi, B. (2020). You are so embarrassing, still, I hate you less! Investigating consumers' brand embarrassment and brand hate. *Journal of Brand Management*, 27(1), 93-107.

Brand emotion

Definition: Brand emotion can be defined as a complex state of feeling to a brand and its related activities resulting from psychological and physical changes that affect thought and behaviour.

> Source: Wong, T. C., Haddoud Mohamed, Y., Kwok, Y. K. & He, H. (2018). Examining the key determinants towards online pro-brand and anti-brand community citizenship behaviours: A two-stage approach. *Industrial Management & Data Systems*, 118(4), 850-872.

Brand endorsement

Definition (1): Brand endorsement is proposed to be more crucial as favorable word-of-mouth communications can be very important in competitive markets. Brand endorsement is associated with advocating a brand to family, friends and other consumers.

Source: Kim, S.-H., Kim, M. & Lee, S. (2019). The consumer value-based brand citizenship behavior model: Evidence from local and global coffee businesses. *Journal of Hospitality Marketing & Management, 28*(4), 472-490.

Definition (2): Brand endorsement involves recommending and advocating the brand to others, such as customers, friends, and family.

Source: Nyadzayo, M. W., Matanda, M. J. & Ewing, M. T. (2016). Franchisee-based brand equity: The role of brand relationship quality and brand citizenship behavior. *Industrial Marketing Management, 52*, 163-174.

Brand energy

Definition: Brand energy refers to the perceived strength of the brand and its ability to act (i.e., power), its capacity to take control (i.e., drive), and to keep going or moving (changing and adapting; i.e., momentum).

Source: Baxter, S. M. & Ilicic, J. (2018). May the force drag your dynamic logo: The brand work-energy effect. *International Journal of Research in Marketing, 35*(3), 509-523.

Brand engagement

Definition (1): Brand engagement can be defined as a psychological state that occurs by virtue of interactive, co-creative customer experiences with a focal agent/object (e.g. a brand).

Source: Bento, M., Martinez, L. M. & Martinez, L. F. (2018). Brand engagement and search for brands on social media: Comparing Generations X and Y in Portugal. *Journal of Retailing and Consumer Services, 43*, 234-241.

Definition (2): Brand engagement has been conceptualized to compose mainly of emotional, cognitive and social engagement.

Source: Xi, N. & Hamari, J. (2020). Does gamification affect brand engagement and equity? A study in online brand communities. *Journal of Business Research, 109*, 449-460.

Definition (3): Brand engagement is defined as the propensity of individuals to incorporate brands as part of their self-concept (i.e., how they see themselves).

Source: Jiménez-Castillo, D. & Sánchez-Fernández, R. (2019). The role of digital influencers in brand recommendation: Examining their impact on engagement, expected value and purchase intention. *International Journal of Information Management, 49*, 366-376.

Definition (4): Brand engagement indicates that consumers are likely to use brands to present self-concept and can enhance consumers' cognitive responses (brand awareness) affective responses (brand associations).

Source: Lee Crystal, T. & Hsieh Sara, H. (2019). Engaging consumers in mobile instant messaging: the role of cute branded emoticons. *Journal of Product & Brand Management, 28*(7), 849-863.

Brand engagement platform

Definition: Brand engagement platform is a physical or digital interactional assemblage of persons (entailing other consumers, company employees, partners, and other stakeholders), artifacts (including data), interfaces, and processes, whose design intensifies brand relationships.

Source: Ramaswamy, V. & Ozcan, K. (2016). Brand value co-creation in a digitalized world: An integrative framework and research implications. *International Journal of Research in Marketing, 33*(1), 93-106.

Brand enthusiasm

Definition: Brand enthusiasm is related to engaging in additional brand developing initiatives, such as involving in marketing actions through sponsorships or charity opportunities, sharing customer opinions that reinforce first-rate branding options. Brand enthusiasm involves taking extra initiatives, such as local marketing through charity events and sponsorships. The expression of brand enthusiasm by individuals may include passing on brand-related customer feedback.

Source: Kim, S.-H., Kim, M. & Lee, S. (2019). The consumer value-based brand citizenship behavior model: Evidence from local and global coffee businesses. *Journal of Hospitality Marketing & Management, 28*(4), 472-490.

brand entification

Definition: Brand entification is an outcome of interactions among brands and users which produce the following attribution: The brand is not just a human who speaks and responds, but a lovable celebrity.

Source: Sashittal, H. C., Hodis, M. & Sriramachandramurthy, R. (2015). Entifying your brand among Twitter-using millennials. *Business Horizons, 58*(3), 325-333.

Brand entretainment content

Definition: Brand entertaining content refers to the posts related to a brand or company or product to entertain the members. Entertainment has four main activities associated: relaxation or escape.

Source: Jayasingh, S. (2019). Consumer brand engagement in social networking sites and its effect on brand loyalty. *Cogent Business & Management, 6*(1), 1698793.

Brand equity

Definition (1): Brand equity refers to the incremental utility or value added to a product from its brand name.

> Source: Henderson, I. L., Tsui, K. W. H., Ngo, T., Gilbey, A. & Avis, M. (2019). Airline brand choice in a duopolistic market: The case of New Zealand. *Transportation Research Part A: Policy and Practice, 121,* 147-163.

Definition (2): Brand equity refers to the differential effect of brand knowledge on a consumer's response to the marketing of a brand and occurs when a consumer is familiar with and loyal to a brand and holds favourable, strong and unique brand associations.

> Source: Napoli, J., Dickinson-Delaporte, S. & Beverland, M. B. (2016). The brand authenticity continuum: strategic approaches for building value. *Journal of Marketing Management, 32*(13-14), 1201-1229.

Definition (3): Brand equity refers to the strength of a brand in customers' minds. Brand equity consists of five categories of brand assets and liabilities: loyalty, brand awareness, perceived quality, brand associations, and other proprietary assets.

> Source: Lee, J. L.-M., Siu, N. Y.-M. & Zhang, T. J.-F. (2020). Does Brand Equity Always Work? A Study of the Moderating Effect of Justice Perceptions and Consumer Attribution Towards Chinese Consumers. *Journal of International Consumer Marketing, 32*(1), 69-81.

Definition (4): Brand equity is the differential preference and response to marketing efforts that a product obtains because of its brand.

> Source: Heitmann, M., Landwehr, J. R., Schreiner, T. F. & van Heerde, H. J. (2020). Leveraging Brand Equity for Effective Visual Product Design. *Journal of Marketing Research, 57*(2), 257-277.

Definition (5): Brand equity considers the customer's subjective and intangible assessment of a brand, above and beyond its objectively perceived value.

> Source: Gao, L., Melero-Polo, I. & Sese, F. J. (2020). Customer Equity Drivers, Customer Experience Quality, and Customer Profitability in Banking Services: The Moderating Role of Social Influence. *Journal of Service Research, 23*(2), 174-193.

Definition (6): Brand equity can be categorized as firm-based brand equity, employee-based brand equity, and consumer-based brand equity.

> Source: Sagynbekova, S., Ince, E., Ogunmokun, O. A., Olaoke, R. O. & Ukeje, U. E. (2021). Social media communication and higher education brand equity: The mediating role of eWOM. *Journal of Public Affairs, n/a*(n/a), e2112.

Definition (7): Brand equity refers to the value of a product solely due to its brand name and perceptions of that brand from a consumer's perspective.

> **Source:** Stockman, S., Van Hoye, G. & da Motta Veiga, S. (2020). Negative word-of-mouth and applicant attraction: The role of employer brand equity. *Journal of Vocational Behavior, 118*, 103368.

Definition (8): Brand equity is defined as the differential effect of brand knowledge on response to the brand's marketing efforts.

> **Source:** Hyun, M. Y. & Kim, H.-C. (2020). Refinement and Validation of a Multidimensional Destination Brand Equity Scale for Inbound and Outbound Chinese Travelers: A Cross-National Perspective. *Journal of Travel Research, 59*(8), 1522-1552.

Definition (9): The concept of brand equity first appeared in the 1980s, closely associated with financial considerations whereby brand equity is estimated based on the incremental cash flows and asset values accrued to a brand. Aaker (1991) considered brand equity to be a set of assets and liabilities associated with the brand name and symbology that can be managed in order to create value. Keller (1993) bases his definition of brand equity on brand knowledge in terms of its awareness (activated through recall and recognition in the case of product absence or presence respectively), as well as brand associations (namely characteristics, benefits).

> **Source:** González-Mansilla, Ó., Berenguer-Contrí, G. & Serra-Cantallops, A. (2019). The impact of value co-creation on hotel brand equity and customer satisfaction. *Tourism Management, 75*, 51-65.

Definition (10): Customer-based brand equity is the additional value provided by a brand name to a product or service, manifests through cognitive and behavioral preferences such as the brand's perceived level of distinctiveness within the service category.

> **Source:** Wu, L., King, C. A., Lu, L. & Guchait, P. (2020). Hospitality aesthetic labor management: Consumers' and prospective employees' perspectives of hospitality brands. *International Journal of Hospitality Management, 87*, 102373.

Definition (11): Consumer-based brand equity refers to a set of perceptions, attitudes, knowledge, and behaviors on the part of consumers... that allows a brand to earn greater volume.

> **Source:** Bazi, S., Filieri, R. & Gorton, M. (2020). Customers' motivation to engage with luxury brands on social media. *Journal of Business Research, 112*, 223-235.

Definition (12): Customer-based brand equity is the driving force for stimulating incremental financial gains for the firm and consists of brand loyalty and awareness

> Source: Xi, N. & Hamari, J. (2020). Does gamification affect brand engagement and equity? A study in online brand communities. *Journal of Business Research*, *109*, 449-460.

Definition (13): Brand equity is defined as assets and liabilities, including brand awareness, loyalty, perceived quality and brand associations linked to a brand's name and symbol that adds to (or subtracts from) the value provided by a product or service to a firm.

> Source: Chekalina, T., Fuchs, M. & Lexhagen, M. (2018). Customer-Based Destination Brand Equity Modeling: The Role of Destination Resources, Value for Money, and Value in Use. *Journal of Travel Research*, *57*(1), 31-51.

Brand ethereality

Definition: Brand ethereality is defined here as the ability of a brand to induce, through their social media posts, customers to imagine ideal or fabulous states.

> Source: Bazi, S., Filieri, R. & Gorton, M. (2020). Customers' motivation to engage with luxury brands on social media. *Journal of Business Research*, *112*, 223-235.

Brand ethicality

Definition: Brand ethicality can be conceptualized as perception of the brand as being honest, responsible, and accountable toward various stakeholders.

> Source: Das, G., Agarwal, J., Malhotra, N. K. & Varshneya, G. (2019). Does brand experience translate into brand commitment?: A mediated-moderation model of brand passion and perceived brand ethicality. *Journal of Business Research*, *95*, 479-490.

Brand evaluations

Definition: Consumers' brand evaluations are defined as customers' general affective assessment of a brand.

> Source: Wu, L., King, C. A., Lu, L. & Guchait, P. (2020). Hospitality aesthetic labor management: Consumers' and prospective employees' perspectives of hospitality brands. *International Journal of Hospitality Management*, *87*, 102373.

Brand evangelism

Definition (1): Brand evangelism refers to an active behavioral and vocal support of a brand such as disseminating positive brand information and convincing others.

> Source: Kang, J., Kwun, D. J. & Hahm, J. J. (2020). Turning Your Customers into Brand Evangelists: Evidence from Cruise Travelers. *Journal of Quality Assurance in Hospitality & Tourism*, *21*(6), 617-643.

Definition (2): Brand evangelism transcends positive WOM communication behaviour as it includes the overt behaviour of intensely and actively disseminating brand-related experience to others and attempting to recruit others to use the brands.

>Source: Nyadzayo, M. W., Leckie, C. & Johnson, L. W. (2020). The impact of relational drivers on customer brand engagement and brand outcomes. *Journal of Brand Management, 27*(5), 561-578.

Brand exclusivity

Definition: Brand exclusivity refers to uniqueness, distinction, and creativity related to the brand.

>Source: Roux, E., Tafani, E. & Vigneron, F. (2017). Values associated with luxury brand consumption and the role of gender. *Journal of Business Research, 71*, 102-113.

Brand experience

Definition (1): Brand experience is defined as subjective, internal consumer responses (sensations, feelings, and cognitions) and behavioral responses evoked by brand-related stimuli that are part of a brand's design and identity, packaging, communications, and environments.

>Source: Kumar, V. & Kaushik, A. K. (2020). Does experience affect engagement? Role of destination brand engagement in developing brand advocacy and revisit intentions. *Journal of Travel & Tourism Marketing, 37*(3), 332-346.

Definition (2): Brand experience refers to consumers' responses triggered by brand-related stimuli that constitute a major part of a brand (e.g., brand name, logo, packaging, advertisements, websites, etc.).

>Source: Kang, J., Kwun, D. J. & Hahm, J. J. (2020). Turning Your Customers into Brand Evangelists: Evidence from Cruise Travelers. *Journal of Quality Assurance in Hospitality & Tourism, 21*(6), 617-643.

Definition (3): Brand experiences are related to sensations, feelings, cognitions and behaviour which are evoked by a brand related stimulus.

>Source: Stach, J. (2019). Meaningful experiences: an embodied cognition perspective on brand meaning co-creation. *Journal of Brand Management, 26*(3), 317-331.

Brand experiential satisfaction

Definition: Brand experiential satisfaction is defined as the result of consumers' overall evaluation of content based on their experience of purchasing branded products.

>Source: Wu, H.-C. & Chang, Y.-Y. (2019). What drives brand supportive intentions? *Marketing Intelligence & Planning, 37*(5), 497-512.

Brand expertise

Definition (1): Brand expertise denotes consumers' perceptions of the ability of a brand to keep and deliver its promises

> **Source:** Zhang, B., Ritchie, B., Mair, J. & Driml, S. (2019). Is the Airline Trustworthy? The Impact of Source Credibility on Voluntary Carbon Offsetting. *Journal of Travel Research*, 58(5), 715-731.

Definition (2): Brand expertise is viewed as customer perception toward the brand to be skilful and knowledgeable.

> **Source:** Nyadzayo, M. W., Leckie, C. & Johnson, L. W. (2020). The impact of relational drivers on customer brand engagement and brand outcomes. *Journal of Brand Management*, 27(5), 561-578.

Brand exposure

Definition: Brand exposure is the time and exposure frequency that a consumer is in contact with a brand.

> **Source:** Kwon, H. & Shin Jae, E. (2019). Effects of brand exposure time duration and frequency on image transfer in sport sponsorship. *International Journal of Sports Marketing and Sponsorship*, 21(1), 170-190.

Brand extension

Definition: Brand extension is regarded as a fundamental business strategy and is defined as the use of an established brand name for the introduction of new products or services.

> **Source:** Ahn, J., Park, J. K. & Hyun, H. (2018). Luxury product to service brand extension and brand equity transfer. *Journal of Retailing and Consumer Services*, 42, 22-28.

Brand failure

Definition: Brand failure is related to a negative brand performance or information.

> **Source:** Cheng, S. Y. Y., White, T. B. & Chaplin, L. N. (2012). The effects of self-brand connections on responses to brand failure: A new look at the consumer–brand relationship. *Journal of Consumer Psychology*, 22(2), 280-288.

Brand familiarity

Definition: Brand familiarity is defined as the number of direct or indirect experiences related to the brand that has been accumulated by the consumer and is directly related to the amount of time that customers spend processing brand information.

Source: Hickman, E., Kharouf, H. & Sekhon, H. (2020). An omnichannel approach to retailing: demystifying and identifying the factors influencing an omnichannel experience. *The International Review of Retail, Distribution and Consumer Research, 30*(3), 266-288.

Brand fan page

Definition: Brand fan pages are public social media profiles created and managed by companies to promote corporate brands and engage existing and potential customers.

Source: Tang, Z., Chen, L. & Gillenson, M. L. (2019). Understanding brand fan page followers' discontinuance motivations: A mixed-method study. *Information & Management, 56*(1), 94-108.

Brand fan page discontinuance

Definition: Brand fan page discontinuance is defined as the follower's intention to remove a brand fan page from his or her following list and no longer wish to receive updates from the Brand fan page.

Source: Tang, Z., Chen, L. & Gillenson, M. L. (2019). Understanding brand fan page followers' discontinuance motivations: A mixed-method study. *Information & Management, 56*(1), 94-108.

Brand feelings

Definition: Brand feelings are emotional reactions to the brand such as excitement and security.

Source: Woo, H., Jung, S. & Jin, B. E. (2020). How far can brands go to defend themselves? The extent of negative publicity impact on proactive consumer behaviors and brand equity. *Business Ethics: A European Review, 29*(1), 193-211.

Brand fidelity

Definition: Brand fidelity, that is centred on consumer actions and thoughts, which exemplify active participation in the maintenance of strong consumer/brand relationships. Defined as the consumer's faithfulness to a brand partner manifested through various behaviours.

Source: Grace, D., Ross, M. & King, C. (2018). Brand fidelity: a relationship maintenance perspective. *Journal of Brand Management, 25*(6), 577-590.

Brand fit

Definition (1): Brand fit is defined as a perceived similarity of two entities – brand and other entity.

Source: Nabec, L., Pras, B. & Laurent, G. (2016). Temporary brand–retailer alliance model: the routes to purchase intentions for selective brands and mass retailers. *Journal of Marketing Management, 32*(7-8), 595-627.

Definition (2): Brand fit is conceptualized by two brands when they are perceived as congruent.

> Source: Stumpf, C. & Baum, M. (2016). Customer Referral Reward–Brand–Fit: A Schema Congruity Perspective. *Psychology & Marketing*, *33*(7), 542-558.

Brand forgiveness

Definition (1): Brand forgiveness is defined to the degree to which an individual is tolerant of and provides support to a brand partner in times of price and performance variations.

> Source: Grace, D., Ross, M. & King, C. (2018). Brand fidelity: a relationship maintenance perspective. *Journal of Brand Management*, *25*(6), 577-590.

Definition (2): Brand forgiveness is defined as an act that tempers justice with mercy with regard to the brand. Forgiving a brand is the tendency to abstain from taking punitive action against the brand, and instead release it from its debt.

> Source: Schnebelen, S. & Bruhn, M. (2018). An appraisal framework of the determinants and consequences of brand happiness. *Psychology & Marketing*, *35*(2), 101-119.

Brand functional congruity

Definition: Brand functional congruity can be defined as the match between consumers' expectations toward utilitarian (functional) product attributes and their perceptions of how the brand is perceived within these attributes.

> Source: Sop, S. A. & Kozak, N. (2019). Effects of brand personality, self-congruity and functional congruity on hotel brand loyalty. *Journal of Hospitality Marketing & Management*, *28*(8), 926-956.

Brand functionality

Definition: Brand functionality refers to the extent to which consumers consider that a brand produces goods or services that can adequately perform the function for which they were created.

> Source: Mohan, M., Jiménez Fernando, R., Brown Brian, P. & Cantrell, C. (2017). Brand skill: linking brand functionality with consumer-based brand equity. *Journal of Product & Brand Management*, *26*(5), 477-491.

Brand gender

Definition: Brand gender refers to the set of human personality traits associated with masculinity and femininity applicable to brands".

> Source: Azar Salim, L., Aimé, I. & Ulrich, I. (2018). Brand gender-bending: The impact of an endorsed brand strategy on consumers' evaluation of gendered mixed-target brands. *European Journal of Marketing*, *52*(7/8), 1598-1624.

Brand gender perception change
Definition: Brand gender perception change is defined as the perceived distance between the gender of the newly created brand system and the gender of the master brand.

> **Source:** Azar Salim, L., Aimé, I. & Ulrich, I. (2018). Brand gender-bending: The impact of an endorsed brand strategy on consumers' evaluation of gendered mixed-target brands. *European Journal of Marketing*, 52(7/8), 1598-1624.

Brand genericization
Definition: Brand genericization refers to a largely involuntary linguistic and social process whereby the brand name tends to become the generic name for the category of products.

> **Source:** Cova, B. & Paranque, B. (2016). Value slippage in brand transformation: a conceptualization. *Journal of Product & Brand Management*, 25(1), 3-10.

Brand globality
Definition: Brand globality is defined as brand widely recognized as global.

> **Source:** Gupta, S., Gallear, D., Rudd, J. & Foroudi, P. (2020). The impact of brand value on brand competitiveness. *Journal of Business Research*, 112, 210-222.

Brand globalness
Definition: Brand globalness is defined as the extent to which consumers believe that a brand is marketed in multiple countries and is recognized as global in these countries.

> **Source:** Halkias, G., Davvetas, V. & Diamantopoulos, A. (2016). The interplay between country stereotypes and perceived brand globalness/localness as drivers of brand preference. *Journal of Business Research*, 69(9), 3621-3628.

Brand goal-congruence
Definition: Brand goal-congruence is defined as the extent to which the goals of a brand are aligned and consistent with the consumer's goals. Brand goal congruence is related to the brand's capacity to achieve the consumer's goals.

> **Source:** Schnebelen, S. & Bruhn, M. (2018). An appraisal framework of the determinants and consequences of brand happiness. *Psychology & Marketing*, 35(2), 101-119.

Brand goodwill
Definition: Brand goodwill refers to a brand intangible asset.

> **Source:** Chan, T. Y., Narasimhan, C. & Yoon, Y. (2017). Advertising and price competition in a manufacturer-retailer channel. *International Journal of Research in Marketing, 34*(3), 694-716.

Brand governance

Definition: Brand governance refers to a system of building a brand that is guided by the vision, mission and values of an organization and that systematically nurtures a brand value to become and remain a long-term strategic asset.

> **Source:** Taks, M., Seguin, B., Naraine, M. L., Thompson, A., Parent, M. M. & Hoye, R. (2020). Brand governance practices in Canadian national sport organizations: an exploratory study. *European Sport Management Quarterly, 20*(1), 10-29.

Brand happiness

Definition: Brand happiness is defined as the positive feelings of a consumer for the use of a brand.

> **Source:** Schnebelen, S. & Bruhn, M. (2018). An appraisal framework of the determinants and consequences of brand happiness. *Psychology & Marketing, 35*(2), 101-119.

Brand hate

Definition (1): Brand hate is a desire for revenge and a desire for avoidance the brand.

> **Source:** Zarantonello, L., Romani, S., Grappi, S. & Bagozzi Richard, P. (2016). Brand hate. *Journal of Product & Brand Management, 25*(1), 11-25.

Definition (2): Brand hate is an intense negative emotional affect towards the brand.

> **Source:** Sheraz, A. & Sharizal, b. H. (2018). The moderating effect of brand recovery on brand hate and desire for reconciliation: A PLS-MGA approach. *International Journal of Business and Society* 19(3):833-850

Brand heritage

Definition (1): Brand heritage is defned as a dimension of a brand's identity found in its track record, longevity, core values, use of symbols and particularly the organizational belief that history is important.

> **Source:** Nguyen, T.-T. & Grohmann, B. (2020). The influence of passion/determination and external disadvantage on consumer responses to brand biographies. *Journal of Brand Management, 27*(4), 452-465.

Definition (2): Brand heritage is defined as the perceived anchoring of the brand to its tradition.

> Source: Fritz, K., Schoenmueller, V. & Bruhn, M. (2017). Authenticity in branding – exploring antecedents and consequences of brand authenticity. *European Journal of Marketing*, 51(2), 324-348.

Brand high status

Definition: Brand High Status is a brand associated with high social class, prestige and sophistication.

> Source: Warren, C., Batra, R., Loureiro, S. M. C. & Bagozzi, R. P. (2019). Brand Coolness. *Journal of Marketing*, 83(5), 36-56.

Brand hypocrisy

Definition: Brand hypocrisy is defined as a brand perceived as intentionally projecting false or unrealistic appearances, thereby implying the dissimulation or manipulation of attributes, motivations or beliefs.

> Source: Guèvremont, A. (2019). Brand hypocrisy from a consumer perspective: scale development and validation. *Journal of Product & Brand Management*, 28(5), 598-613.

Brand icon

Definition: Brand icon is defined as a graphic image, illustration or symbol that represents a concept.

> Source: Bresciani, S. & Del Ponte, P. (2017). New brand logo design: customers' preference for brand name and icon. *Journal of Brand Management*, 24(5), 375-390.

Brand identification

Definition: Brand identification can be defined as the level of perception to which brand community members attach themselves to the brand's success.

> Source: Wong, T. C., Haddoud Mohamed, Y., Kwok, Y. K. & He, H. (2018). Examining the key determinants towards online pro-brand and anti-brand community citizenship behaviours: A two-stage approach. *Industrial Management & Data Systems*, 118(4), 850-872.

Brand identity

Definition: Brand identity represents the internal perspective of what the brand is.

> Source: Dean, D., Arroyo-Gamez, R. E., Punjaisri, K. & Pich, C. (2016). Internal brand co-creation: The experiential brand meaning cycle in higher education. *Journal of Business Research*, 69(8), 3041-3048.

Brand image

Definition (1): Brand image is described as the network of brand-related information that consumers retain in memory, which captures the perceptions and preferences for a brand.

> **Source:** Pourazad, N., Stocchi, L. & Pare, V. (2019). Brand attribute associations, emotional consumer-brand relationship and evaluation of brand extensions. *Australasian Marketing Journal (AMJ)*, 27(4), 249-260.

Definition (2): Brand image reflects how the external market perceives the brand.

> **Source:** Dean, D., Arroyo-Gamez, R. E., Punjaisri, K. & Pich, C. (2016). Internal brand co-creation: The experiential brand meaning cycle in higher education. *Journal of Business Research*, 69(8), 3041-3048.

Definition (3): Brand image is the perceptions about a brand as reflected by the brand associations held in consumer memory.

> **Source:** Baumann, C., Hamin, H. & Chong, A. (2015). The role of brand exposure and experience on brand recall—Product durables vis-à-vis FMCG. *Journal of Retailing and Consumer Services*, 23, 21-31.

Definition (4): Brand image has been considered as the reasoned or emotional perceptions consumers attach to specific brands

> **Source:** Cano Guervos, R. A., Frías Jamilena, D. M., Polo Peña, A. I. & Chica Olmo, J. (2020). Influence of Tourist Geographical Context on Customer-Based Destination Brand Equity: An Empirical Analysis. *Journal of Travel Research*, 59(1), 107-119.

Definition (5): Brand image is another consideration of brand knowledge suggested in the literature. Which is conceptualized as perceptions about a brand as revealed by the brand associations retained in the mind of consumers.

> **Source:** Barreda, A. A., Bilgihan, A., Nusair, K. & Okumus, F. (2016). Online branding: Development of hotel branding through interactivity theory. *Tourism Management*, 57, 180-192.

Definition (6): Brand image is identified as the representation of a brand in the consumer's mind or a set of perceptions about a brand, either objective or subjective. Hence, it can be defined as the reasoned or emotional perceptions about a brand.

> **Source:** Han, H., Nguyen, H. N., Song, H., Chua, B.-L., Lee, S. & Kim, W. (2018). Drivers of brand loyalty in the chain coffee shop industry. *International Journal of Hospitality Management*, 72, 86-97.

Brand image congruity

Definition: Brand image congruity is a consumer's perception of the consistency between a particular brand image and his/her own self-image.

Source: Chen-Yu, J., Cho, S. & Kincade, D. (2016). Brand perception and brand repurchase intent in online apparel shopping: An examination of brand experience, image congruence, brand affect, and brand trust. *Journal of Global Fashion Marketing*, 7(1), 30-44.

Brand imitation

Definition: Brand imitation relies on the concept of visual similarity and how consumers may confuse private labels resulting in consumers purchasing the private labels unintentionally.

Source: Aribarg, A. & Schwartz, E. M. (2020). Native Advertising in Online News: Trade-Offs Among Clicks, Brand Recognition, and Website Trustworthiness. *Journal of Marketing Research*, 57(1), 20-34.

Brand inner self expressiveness

Definition: Brand inner self-expressiveness is experienced by a consumer privately and refers to the degree to which one feels that the focal brand is an extension of one's inner self and the brand mirrors what one really is. Brand inner self-expressiveness is experienced by a consumer privately.

Source: Sarkar, A., Sarkar, J. G., Sreejesh, S., Anusree, M. R. & Rishi, B. (2020). You are so embarrassing, still, I hate you less! Investigating consumers' brand embarrassment and brand hate. *Journal of Brand Management*, 27(1), 93-107.

Brand innovativeness

Definition (1): Brand innovativeness is defined as the extent to which consumers perceive a brand as being able to provide new and useful solutions to their needs.

Source: Srivastava, N., Dash Satya, B. & Mookerjee, A. (2015). Antecedents and moderators of brand trust in the context of baby care toiletries. *Journal of Consumer Marketing*, 32(5), 328-340.

Definition (2): Brand innovativeness is defined as consumer's perception of an enduring firm capability that results in novel, creative, and impactful ideas and solutions for the market.

Source: Coelho, F. J. F., Bairrada, C. M. & de Matos Coelho, A. F. (2020). Functional brand qualities and perceived value: The mediating role of brand experience and brand personality. *Psychology & Marketing*, 37(1), 41-55.

Brand integration

Definition: Brand integration refers to the extent to which a firm uses its existing brand, rather than a modified version or even a new brand, to name its innovation.

Source: Patel, C. (2014). Successful service retail channel expansions: The roles of technical and brand integration. *Industrial Marketing Management*, 43(1), 102-112.

Brand integrity

Definition: Brand integrity is a dimension of brand authenticity which signifies the moral purity and responsibility of the brand.

Source: Moulard, J. G., Raggio, R. D. & Folse, J. A. G. (2016). Brand Authenticity: Testing the Antecedents and Outcomes of Brand Management's Passion for its Products. *Psychology & Marketing*, 33(6), 421-436.

Brand interactivity

Definition: Brand interactivity is defined as the assistance offered to customers on social media as well as the space for discussions and the exchange of ideas.

Source: Dabbous, A. & Barakat, K. A. (2020). Bridging the online offline gap: Assessing the impact of brands' social network content quality on brand awareness and purchase intention. *Journal of Retailing and Consumer Services*, 53, 101966.

Brand interest

Definition: Brand interest is defined as the base level of approachability, inquisitiveness, openness, or curiosity that an individual has about a brand.

Source: Shin, H., Eastman, J. K. & Mothersbaugh, D. (2017). The effect of a limited-edition offer following brand dilution on consumer attitudes toward a luxury brand. *Journal of Retailing and Consumer Services*, 38, 59-70.

Brand intimacy

Definition: Brand intimacy expresses the degree of closeness, connectedness, and bonding that the brand shares with its customers. Brand intimacy involves emotional and psychological intimacy.

Source: Srivastava, N., Dash Satya, B. & Mookerjee, A. (2015). Antecedents and moderators of brand trust in the context of baby care toiletries. *Journal of Consumer Marketing*, 32(5), 328-340.

Brand involvement

Definition (1): Brand involvement refers to a motivational state which is defined as a person's perceived relevance of the brand based on intrinsic needs, values, and interests.

Source: Chang, A., Hsieh Sara, H. & Tseng Timmy, H. (2013). Online brand community response to negative brand events: the role of group eWOM. *Internet Research*, 23(4), 486-506.

Definition (2): Brand involvement is a mental state that influences the allocation of cognitive resources to evaluation of an brand, object, decision, or action.

> **Source:** Bian, X. & Haque, S. (2020). Counterfeit versus original patronage: Do emotional brand attachment, brand involvement, and past experience matter? *Journal of Brand Management, 27*(4), 438-451.

Brand jealousy

Definition: Brand jealousy is a strong feeling experienced within the scope of romantic relationship with the brand.

> **Source:** Bıçakcıoğlu, N., Ögel, İ. Y. & İlter, B. (2017). Brand jealousy and willingness to pay premium: The mediating role of materialism. *Journal of Brand Management, 24*(1), 33-48.

Brand knowledge

Definition (1): Brand knowledge has many dimensions, such as awareness, attributes, benefits, images, thoughts, feelings, attitudes and experiences.

> **Source:** Langaro, D., de Fátima Salgueiro, M., Rita, P. & Del Chiappa, G. (2019). Users' Participation in Facebook Brand Pages and Its Influence on Word-of-Mouth: The Role of Brand Knowledge and Brand Relationship. *Journal of Creative Communications, 14*(3), 177-195.

Definition (2): Brand knowledge is defined as a consistent of brand node in consumers' mind to which a diverse set of associations are connected.

> **Source:** Barreda, A. A., Bilgihan, A., Nusair, K. & Okumus, F. (2016). Online branding: Development of hotel branding through interactivity theory. *Tourism Management, 57*, 180-192.

Brand legitimacy

Definition (1): Brand legitimacy describes the consumer brand fit and refers to the brand's degree of integration in the set of values and norms shared by a community.

> **Source:** Fritz, K., Schoenmueller, V. & Bruhn, M. (2017). Authenticity in branding – exploring antecedents and consequences of brand authenticity. *European Journal of Marketing, 51*(2), 324-348.

Definition (2): Brand legitimacy can be defined as the actions of a brand that are desirable, proper, or appropriate within some socially constructed system of norms, values, beliefs, and definitions.

> **Source:** Hu, M., Qiu, P., Wan, F. & Stillman, T. (2018). Love or hate, depends on who's saying it: How legitimacy of brand rejection alters brand preferences. *Journal of Business Research, 90*, 164-170.

Brand licensing

Definition: Brand licensing can be defined as an agreement through which the licensee acquires the right to use the brand name owned by the licensor to manufacture, sell, promote and distribute a product in a defined territory and for an established period of time.

> **Source:** Cardinali, S., Travaglini, M. & Giovannetti, M. (2019). Increasing Brand Orientation and Brand Capabilities Using Licensing: an Opportunity for SMEs in International Markets. *Journal of the Knowledge Economy*, *10*(4), 1808-1830.

Brand localness

Definition (1): Brand localness refers to the extent to which a brand is recognized as a local player and a symbol or icon of the local culture.

> **Source:** Halkias, G., Davvetas, V. & Diamantopoulos, A. (2016). The interplay between country stereotypes and perceived brand globalness/localness as drivers of brand preference. *Journal of Business Research*, *69*(9), 3621-3628.

Definition (2): Brand localness is described as the extent to which a brand is perceived as a player connected with the local country and embedded in its consumption culture.

> **Source:** Sichtmann, C., Davvetas, V. & Diamantopoulos, A. (2019). The relational value of perceived brand globalness and localness. *Journal of Business Research*, *104*, 597-613.

Brand logo

Definition (1): Brand logo is a graphical image or design that is important brand elements that have a direct impact on the brand's reputation. Brand logos are the most salient visual element of a brand, facilitating brand identification and differentiation.

> **Source:** Baxter, S. M. & Ilicic, J. (2018). May the force drag your dynamic logo: The brand work-energy effect. *International Journal of Research in Marketing*, *35*(3), 509-523.

Definition (2): Brand logo refers to the graphic design that companies use to identify themselves and their products, with or without the firm's name.

> **Source:** Bresciani, S. & Del Ponte, P. (2017). New brand logo design: customers' preference for brand name and icon. *Journal of Brand Management*, *24*(5), 375-390.

Brand longevity

Definition: Brand longevity refers to the extent to which consumers perceive that the brand has been in existence for a long period of time.

Source: Moulard, J. G., Raggio, R. D. & Folse, J. A. G. (2016). Brand Authenticity: Testing the Antecedents and Outcomes of Brand Management's Passion for its Products. *Psychology & Marketing, 33*(6), 421-436.

Brand love

Definition (1): Brand love is a consumer's emotional bond with a brand, characterised by the positive evaluation of the brand and declarations of love for the brand.

Source: Pourazad, N., Stocchi, L. & Pare, V. (2019). Brand attribute associations, emotional consumer-brand relationship and evaluation of brand extensions. *Australasian Marketing Journal (AMJ), 27*(4), 249-260.

Definition (2): Brand love can be defined as the degree of passionate emotional attachment a satisfied consumer has for a particular trade name and encompasses a number of affective responses toward the brand, including passion.

Source: Mody, M. & Hanks, L. (2020). Consumption Authenticity in the Accommodations Industry: The Keys to Brand Love and Brand Loyalty for Hotels and Airbnb. *Journal of Travel Research, 59*(1), 173-189.

Definition (3): Brand love refers to the relationship between the consumer and the brand, which is emotional, passionate and formed over time.

Source: Napoli, J., Dickinson-Delaporte, S. & Beverland, M. B. (2016). The brand authenticity continuum: strategic approaches for building value. *Journal of Marketing Management, 32*(13-14), 1201-1229.

Definition (4): Brand love represents the intimate experience of very positive emotion toward a particular brand.

Source: Gómez Suárez, M. (2018). Examining Customer-Brand Relationships: A Critical Approach to Empirical Models on Brand Attachment, Love, and Engagement. *Administrative Sciences, 9.*

Definition: Brand love is defined as the emotional bond and positive feelings that consumers experience when thinking about or using a brand.

Source: Delgado-Ballester, E., Palazón, M. & Peláez, J. (2019). Anthropomorphized vs objectified brands: which brand version is more loved? *European Journal of Management and Business Economics, 29*(2), 150-165.

Brand loyalty

Definition (1): Brand loyalty is defined as the extent of faithfulness of consumers to a particular brand, irrespective of the marketing activities of competitive brands.

Source: Giovanis, A. N. & Athanasopoulou, P. (2018). Consumer-brand relationships and brand loyalty in technology-mediated services. *Journal of Retailing and Consumer Services, 40*, 287-294.

Definition (2): Brand loyalty is as a deeply held commitment to rebuy or repatronize a preferred brand consistently in the future.

Source: Molinillo, S., Japutra, A., Nguyen, B. & Chen Cheng-Hao, S. (2017). Responsible brands vs active brands? An examination of brand personality on brand awareness, brand trust, and brand loyalty. *Marketing Intelligence & Planning, 35*(2), 166-179.

Definition (3): Brand loyalty can be defined as the attachment that a customer has to a brand.

Source: Cano Guervos, R. A., Frías Jamilena, D. M., Polo Peña, A. I. & Chica Olmo, J. (2020). Influence of Tourist Geographical Context on Customer-Based Destination Brand Equity: An Empirical Analysis. *Journal of Travel Research, 59*(1), 107-119.

Definition (4): Brand loyalty is defined as a commitment toward a brand, willingness to pay for the brand, the action of recommending the brand to other people, keeping in touch with the latest news of the brand.

Source: Wahyuni, S. & Fitriani, N. (2017). Brand religiosity aura and brand loyalty in Indonesia Islamic banking. *Journal of Islamic Marketing, 8*(3), 361-372.

Definition (5): Brand loyalty is commonly defined as the biased (non-random) behavioral response expressed over time by some decision-making unit with respect to one or more alternative brands out of a set of brands.

Source: Han, H., Nguyen, H. N., Song, H., Chua, B.-L., Lee, S. & Kim, W. (2018). Drivers of brand loyalty in the chain coffee shop industry. *International Journal of Hospitality Management, 72*, 86-97.

Brand luxuriousness

Definition: Brand luxuriousness is defined as the extent to which a product is conducive to sumptuous living rather than the necessity that entails different facets, such as conspicuousness, uniqueness.

Source: Siew, S.-W., Minor, M. S. & Felix, R. (2018). The influence of perceived strength of brand origin on willingness to pay more for luxury goods. *Journal of Brand Management, 25*(6), 591-605.

Brand management efficiency

Definition: Brand management efficiency is defined as a firm's capability to minimize utilization of resources (inputs) to achieve an optimal result (output) such as brand equity.

Source: Rahman, M., Rodríguez-Serrano, M. Á. & Lambkin, M. (2018). Brand management efficiency and firm value: An integrated resource based and signalling theory perspective. *Industrial Marketing Management, 72*, 112-126.

Brand mascot

Definition: Brand mascot is a brand character that reflects the attribution of human characteristics onto brand things.

Source: Cayla, J. (2013). Brand mascots as organisational totems. *Journal of Marketing Management, 29*(1-2), 86-104.

brand meaning

Definition: Brand meaning, is understood as associations, created through deliberate efforts of the marketer and ascribed to the brand by the consumer.

Source: Stach, J. (2019). Meaningful experiences: an embodied cognition perspective on brand meaning co-creation. *Journal of Brand Management, 26*(3), 317-331.

Brand mianzi

Definition: Brand mianzi represents the individual's reputation and social position in others' eye. Mianzi or Face is a concept that is peculiar to Chinese culture and implies consciousness of glory and shame.

Source: Filieri, R., Lin, Z., D'Antone, S. & Chatzopoulou, E. (2019). A cultural approach to brand equity: the role of brand mianzi and brand popularity in China. *Journal of Brand Management, 26*(4), 376-394.

Brand microblog

Definition: Brand micro-blog is a type of company-initiated online brand community, different from the traditional brand community, micro-blogs can foster ongoing conversations between marketers and followers at every stage of the marketing process: pre-purchase, purchase.

Source: Zhao, H., Su, C. & Hua, Z. (2016). Investigating continuance intention to follow a brand micro-blog:Perceived value and social identification. *Information Development, 32*(5), 1428-1441.

Brand micro-blog identification

Definition: Brand micro-blog identification is defined as the strength of a followers' relationship with the blog or the degree to which they perceive oneness with the blog.

Source: Zhao, H., Su, C. & Hua, Z. (2016). Investigating continuance intention to follow a brand micro-blog:Perceived value and social identification. *Information Development, 32*(5), 1428-1441.

Brand narrative

Definition: Brand Narrative refers to a story, or, in many instances a number of diferent stories regarding the brand.

>**Source:** Rowley, J. & Hanna, S. (2020). Branding destinations: symbolic and narrative representations and co-branding. *Journal of Brand Management, 27*(3), 328-338.

Brand need for cognition

Definition: Brand need for cognition is denoted as a consumer's tendency to engage in and enjoy branding.

>**Source:** Wu, H.-C. & Chang, Y.-Y. (2019). What drives brand supportive intentions? *Marketing Intelligence & Planning, 37*(5), 497-512.

Brand news

Definition: Brand news refers to a customer's interest in seeking and gathering new information about the brand, including new trends, products and events.

>**Source:** Bazi, S., Filieri, R. & Gorton, M. (2020). Customers' motivation to engage with luxury brands on social media. *Journal of Business Research, 112*, 223-235.

Brand nostalgia

Definition: brand nostalgia is defined as the consumer's perception of the nostalgic brand staging.

>**Source:** Fritz, K., Schoenmueller, V. & Bruhn, M. (2017). Authenticity in branding – exploring antecedents and consequences of brand authenticity. *European Journal of Marketing, 51*(2), 324-348.

Brand orientation

Definition (1): Brand orientation was created in market orientation domain and is defined as the brand's orientation that tries not only to satisfy customer wants and needs.

>**Source:** Cardinali, S., Travaglini, M. & Giovannetti, M. (2019). Increasing Brand Orientation and Brand Capabilities Using Licensing: an Opportunity for SMEs in International Markets. *Journal of the Knowledge Economy, 10*(4), 1808-1830.

Definition (2): Brand orientation is an approach in which the process of the organization revolves around the creation, development and protection of brand identity in an ongoing interaction with target customers with the aim of achieving lasting competitive advantages.

>**Source:** Schmidt, H. J. & Baumgarth, C. (2018). Strengthening internal brand equity with brand ambassador programs: development and testing of a success factor model. *Journal of Brand Management, 25*(3), 250-265.

Definition (3): Brand orientation is defined as an approach in which the processes of the organization revolve around the creation, development, and protection of brand identity in an ongoing interaction with target.

> Source: Zhang, J., Jiang, Y., Shabbir, R. & Zhu, M. (2016). How brand orientation impacts B2B service brand equity? An empirical study among Chinese firms. *Journal of Business & Industrial Marketing*, 31(1), 83-98.

Definition (4): Brand orientation is the degree to which an organization views brands and brand management as being critical to their success.

> Source: Iyer, P., Davari, A. & Paswan, A. (2018). Determinants of brand performance: the role of internal branding. *Journal of Brand Management*, 25(3), 202-216.

Brand origin

Definition: Brand origin is viewed as the country which brand is associated with or the headquarters of where the brand's owner is perceived to be located, regardless of where it is manufactured.

> Source: Mandler, T., Bartsch, F. & Han, C. M. (2020). Brand credibility and marketplace globalization: The role of perceived brand globalness and localness. *Journal of International Business Studies*.

Brand page

Definition: Brand pages is also known as a fan page or a brand community. brand pages are an effective platform on which companies and customers can interact.

> Source: Duong, G. H., Wu, W.-Y. & Le, L. H. (2020). The effects of brand page characteristics on customer brand engagement: moderating roles of community involvement and comedy production contents. *Journal of Brand Management*, 27(5), 531-545.

Brand page activity

Definition: Brand page activity is viewed as a perception of actions of a brand page

> Source: Duong, G. H., Wu, W.-Y. & Le, L. H. (2020). The effects of brand page characteristics on customer brand engagement: moderating roles of community involvement and comedy production contents. *Journal of Brand Management*, 27(5), 531-545.

Brand page commitment

Definition: Brand page commitment refers to a customer's strong attachment to and emotional bonds with a brand page and can be built upon superior values derived from the regular posts on the brand page, and also on customers' engagement with the brand page.

> **Source:** Shi, S., Cao, Y., Chen, Y. & Chow, W. S. (2019). How social media brand pages contribute to functional conflict: The central role of commitment. *International Journal of Information Management, 45*, 95-106.

Brand page content quality

Definition: Brand page content quality is the informational quality, which emphasizes the accuracy, completeness, relevance, and timeliness of brand-related information on the brand page.

> **Source:** Duong, G. H., Wu, W.-Y. & Le, L. H. (2020). The effects of brand page characteristics on customer brand engagement: moderating roles of community involvement and comedy production contents. *Journal of Brand Management, 27*(5), 531-545.

Brand page interactivity

Definition: Brand page interactivity refers to a customer's perception that the brand page environment can facilitate the interaction between them, the brand, and other customers of the brand community"

> **Source:** Duong, G. H., Wu, W.-Y. & Le, L. H. (2020). The effects of brand page characteristics on customer brand engagement: moderating roles of community involvement and comedy production contents. *Journal of Brand Management, 27*(5), 531-545.

Brand passion

Definition: Brand passion is a consumer's affective and extremely positive attitude towards a brand typically expressed through feelings of 'excitation, infatuation and obsession' towards the brand.

> **Source:** Pourazad, N., Stocchi, L. & Pare, V. (2019). Brand attribute associations, emotional consumer-brand relationship and evaluation of brand extensions. *Australasian Marketing Journal (AMJ), 27*(4), 249-260.

Brand penetration

Definition: Brand penetration is defined as the proportion of people who buy the brand in relation to people who buy the brand category at least once in the defined period. Brand penetration measures the size of a brand's customer base.

> **Source:** Sitta, D., Faulkner, M. & Stern, P. (2018). What can the brand manager expect from Facebook? *Australasian Marketing Journal (AMJ), 26*(1), 17-22.

Brand perceptions

Definition: Brand perceptions is a multi-dimensional construct which emcompasses experimental, symbolic, emotional/affective, and cognitive dimensions.

> **Source:** Chen-Yu, J., Cho, S. & Kincade, D. (2016). Brand perception and brand repurchase intent in online apparel shopping: An examination of brand experience, image congruence, brand affect, and brand trust. *Journal of Global Fashion Marketing*, 7(1), 30-44.

Brand performance

Definition: Brand performance is viewed as a combination of financial performance measures (such as market share and profitability) and non-financial performance measures that are oriented toward the medium- to long-term maintenance of brands.

> **Source:** Iyer, P., Davari, A. & Paswan, A. (2018). Determinants of brand performance: the role of internal branding. *Journal of Brand Management*, 25(3), 202-216.

Brand personality

Definition (1): Brand personality refers to the set of human traits that consumers related to a brand. Brand personality dimensions are: sincerity, competence, excitement, sophistication, and ruggedness.

> **Source:** Kim, P., Vaidyanathan, R., Chang, H. & Stoel, L. (2018). Using brand alliances with artists to expand retail brand personality. *Journal of Business Research*, 85, 424-433.

Definition (2): Brand personality evolves the relationship over timeker and the new dimensions are: responsibility, activity, aggressiveness, simplicity, and emotionality.

> **Source:** Molinillo, S., Japutra, A., Nguyen, B. & Chen Cheng-Hao, S. (2017). Responsible brands vs active brands? An examination of brand personality on brand awareness, brand trust, and brand loyalty. *Marketing Intelligence & Planning*, 35(2), 166-179.

Brand placement

Definition: Brand placement is a paid product message, aimed at influencing movie and /or television audiences via the planned and unobtrusive entry of a branded product.

> **Source:** Vashisht, D. & Royne, M. B. (2016). Advergame speed influence and brand recall: The moderating effects of brand placement strength and gamers' persuasion knowledge. *Computers in Human Behavior*, 63, 162-169.

Brand placement strength

Definition: Brand placement strength (or brand prominence) as the extent to which the appearance of the brand possesses characteristics designed to make it the central focus of audience attention.

> **Source:** Vashisht, D. & Royne, M. B. (2016). Advergame speed influence and brand recall: The moderating effects of brand placement strength and gamers' persuasion knowledge. *Computers in Human Behavior, 63*, 162-169.

Brand play

Definition: Brand play can be identified when the brand is used as a fodder for parody. It has its roots in culture jamming and the playful creation of parodies.
> **Source:** Kristal, S., Baumgarth, C. & Henseler, J. (2018). Brand play versus Brand attack: the subversion of brand meaning in non-collaborative co-creation by professional artists and consumer activists. *Journal of Product & Brand Management, 27*, 334-347.

Brand polarization

Definition: Brand polarization is defined as an affective phenomenon where beliefs and emotions of a significant number of people induce a simultaneous move to the extremes involving passionate positive and negative feelings and convictions towards the brand.

> **Source:** Osuna Ramírez Sergio, A., Veloutsou, C. & Morgan-Thomas, A. (2019). I hate what you love: brand polarization and negativity towards brands as an opportunity for brand management. *Journal of Product & Brand Management, 28*(5), 614-632.

Brand popularity

Definition: Brand popularity is defined as people's recognizement to brands actions and is a consequence of market acceptance and brand goodwill over time that has a positive impact on brand image.

> **Source:** Luan, J., Shan, W., Wang, Y. & Xiao, J. (2019). How easy-to-process information influences consumers over time: Online review vs. brand popularity. *Computers in Human Behavior, 97*, 193-201.

Brand portfolio

Definition: Brand portfolio refers to the set of brands that a company has.

> **Source:** Nguyen, H. T., Zhang, Y. & Calantone, R. J. (2018). Brand portfolio coherence: Scale development and empirical demonstration. *International Journal of Research in Marketing, 35*(1), 60-80.

Brand portfolio coherence

Definition: Brand portfolio coherence is the perception that brands in a portfolio share a common underlying logic of features as reflected in the design, personality, and status of the sub-brands in that portfolio.

> Source: Nguyen, H. T., Zhang, Y. & Calantone, R. J. (2018). Brand portfolio coherence: Scale development and empirical demonstration. *International Journal of Research in Marketing*, 35(1), 60-80.

Brand portfolio fit

Definition: Brand portfolio fit is defined as the perceived fit between product brands in a brand portfolio.

> Source: Brunner, C. B. & Baum, M. (2020). The impact of brand portfolios on organizational attractiveness. *Journal of Business Research*, 106, 182-195.

Brand portfolio strength

Definition: Brand portfolio strength describes the extent of an individual's familiarity with the product brands within the portfolio.

> Source: Brunner, C. B. & Baum, M. (2020). The impact of brand portfolios on organizational attractiveness. *Journal of Business Research*, 106, 182-195.

Brand positioning

Definition (1): Brand positioning is the act of designing a company's offer and image so that the brand occupies a distinct and valued place in the target customer's mind.

> Source: Zhang, M., Li, L., Ye, Y., Qin, K. & Zhong, J. (2020). The effect of brand anthropomorphism, brand distinctiveness, and warmth on brand attitude: A mediated moderation model. *Journal of Consumer Behaviour*, 19(5), 523-536.

Definition (2): Brand positioning refers to a brand world in consumers' mind.

> Source: Kumar, S. M. & Jayasimha, K. R. (2019). Brand verbs: brand synonymity and brand leadership. *Journal of Brand Management*, 26(2), 110-125.

Brand post

Definition: Brand posts are the publications on social networks by anyone about the brand.

> Source: Wang, S. S., Lin, Y.-C. & Liang, T.-P. (2018). Posts that attract millions of fans: The effect of brand-post congruence. *Electronic Commerce Research and Applications*, 28, 73-85.

Brand power

Definition: Brand power can be associated with the sense of belonging and proximity to the brand, associated with the challenging sense of common rules and behaviors of the brand and associated with the fame of the brands.

Source: Nobar, H. & Rostamzadeh, R. (2018). The impact of customer satisfaction, customer experience and customer loyalty on brand power: Empirical evidence from hotel industry. *Journal of Business Economics and Management, 19*, 417-430.

Brand predictability

Definition: Brand predictability refers to the ability of consumers to anticipate a brand's future actions and depends on consumers' knowledge of the brand's past behavior, and the degree to which that behavior is consistent and stable.

Source: Srivastava, N., Dash Satya, B. & Mookerjee, A. (2015). Antecedents and moderators of brand trust in the context of baby care toiletries. *Journal of Consumer Marketing, 32*(5), 328-340.

brand preference

Definition: Brand preference refers to the customer choice of a specific brand over a similar product.

Source: Zameer, H., Wang, Y. & Yasmeen, H. (2019). Transformation of firm innovation activities into brand effect. *Marketing Intelligence & Planning, 37*(2), 226-240.

Brand prestige

Definition: Brand prestige is the relatively high status of a product associated with a brand which is usually established by the know-how, intrinsic worth, or precious image of the specific brand.

Source: Vuong, B. N. & Khanh Giao, H. N. (2020). The Impact of Perceived Brand Globalness on Consumers' Purchase Intention and the Moderating Role of Consumer Ethnocentrism: An Evidence from Vietnam. *Journal of International Consumer Marketing, 32*(1), 47-68.

Brand pride

Definition: Brand pride is defined as the experienced pleasure of being associated with a brand.

Source: Taute Harry, A., Sierra Jeremy, J., Carter Larry, L. & Maher Amro, A. (2017). A sequential process of brand tribalism, brand pride and brand attitude to explain purchase intention: a cross-continent replication study. *Journal of Product & Brand Management, 26*(3), 239-250.

Brand prominence

Definition: Brand prominence refers to the ease and frequency with which a brand is evoked to the top of the mind and, as such, reflects the salience of a customer's psychological connection with the brand.

Source: Badrinarayanan, V. & Becerra, E. P. (2019). Antecedents and consequences of shoppers' attitude toward branded store-within-stores: An exploratory framework. *Journal of Business Research, 105*, 189-200.

Brand promise

Definition: Brand promise is widely recognised that consistent fulfilment of the brand expectations and encapsulates the functional and emotional values, qualities, and experiences, associated with tangible goods and intangible services offered by the brand.

> **Source:** (Karanges, E., Johnston, K. A., Lings, I. & Beatson, A. T. (2018). Brand signalling: An antecedent of employee brand understanding. *Journal of Brand Management*, 25(3), 235-249.

Brand prototype

Definition: Brand prototype is the consumer overall knowledge that is beyond the structural features of brand embedded with the thinking of a consumer that stimulates the whole process of brand evaluation and selection.

> **Source:** Zameer, H., Wang, Y. & Yasmeen, H. (2019). Transformation of firm innovation activities into brand effect. *Marketing Intelligence & Planning*, 37(2), 226-240.

Brand psychological ownership

Definition: Brand psychological ownership is a mental state where the individuals feel that the target of ownership or a part of it is theirs and this state results in favourable behaviours towards the object and enhanced valuation of the target object (brand).

> **Source:** Kumar, J. & Nayak Jogendra, K. (2019). Brand engagement without brand ownership: a case of non-brand owner community members. *Journal of Product & Brand Management*, 28(2), 216-230.

Brand public

Definition: Brand publics are social formations (not structured) that are not based interaction but on a continuous focus of brand interest and brand mediation.

> **Source:** Arvidsson, A. & Caliandro, A. (2015). Brand Public. *Journal of Consumer Research*, 42(5), 727-748.

Brand quality

Definition: Brand quality is defined as perceived overall superiority of a product that compares customers' expectations and perceived performance, thereby reflecting an overall judgment toward the excellence of service delivery.

> **Source:** Chekalina, T., Fuchs, M. & Lexhagen, M. (2018). Customer-Based Destination Brand Equity Modeling: The Role of Destination Resources, Value for Money, and Value in Use. *Journal of Travel Research*, 57(1), 31-51.

Brand recall

Definition (1): Brand recall is a consumer's ability to retrieve a brand when given the product category, the needs fulfilled by the category, or some other type of probe as a cue.

> **Source:** Baumann, C., Hamin, H. & Chong, A. (2015). The role of brand exposure and experience on brand recall—Product durables vis-à-vis FMCG. *Journal of Retailing and Consumer Services, 23*, 21-31.

Definition (2): Brand recall is how well consumers remember the brand's products.

> **Source:** Rashid, R. M., Rashid, Q. u. A., Nawaz, M. A. & Akhtar, S. (2019). Young Chinese consumers' brand perception; the role of mianzi as moderator. *Journal of Public Affairs, 19*(4), e1930.

Definition (3): Brand recall means when consumers see a product, can they recall a brand name exactly.

> **Source:** Cuomo, M., Foroudi, P., Tortora, D., Hussain, S. & Melewar, T. C. (2019). Celebrity Endorsement and the Attitude Towards Luxury Brands for Sustainable Consumption. *Sustainability, 11*, 6791.

Brand recognition

Definition (1): Brand recognition is related to the capacity whether consumers the ability to identify a brand, when there is a brand cue.

> **Source:** Cuomo, M., Foroudi, P., Tortora, D., Hussain, S. & Melewar, T. C. (2019). Celebrity Endorsement and the Attitude Towards Luxury Brands for Sustainable Consumption. *Sustainability, 11*, 6791.

Definition (2): Brand recognition is the extent to which the general public (or an organization's target market) is able to identify a brand by its attributes.

> **Source:** Hussein, R. & Hassan, S. (2018). Antecedents of Global Brand Purchase Likelihood: Exploring the Mediating Effect of Quality, Prestige and Familiarity. *Journal of International Consumer Marketing, 30*(5), 288-303.

Brand recovery

Definition: Brand recovery consists in three strategies: apology, compensation and explanation.

> **Source:** Sheraz, A. & Sharizal, b. H. (2018). The moderating effect of brand recovery on brand hate and desire for reconciliation: A PLS-MGA approach. *International Journal of Business and Society*, Vol. 19 No. 3

Brand regeneration.

Definition: Brand regeneration is known as brand rejuvenation which consists in refreshes the brand or creates a new brand from the existing brand.

>   **Source:** Cova, B. & Paranque, B. (2016). Value slippage in brand transformation: a conceptualization. *Journal of Product & Brand Management, 25*(1), 3-10.

Brand regret

Definition: Brand regret is defined as an emotion that can be experienced when a brand is realized or imagined as more beneficial than if it had been decided differently. Regret is defined as a counterfactual emotion due to the accompanying brand cognitive processes.

>   **Source:** Wu, H.-C. & Chang, Y.-Y. (2019). What drives brand supportive intentions? *Marketing Intelligence & Planning, 37*(5), 497-512.

Brand rejection

Definition: Brand rejection is the rejecting messages or actions originating from consumers and targeted towards companies or brands, such as anti-consumption behavior or consumers boycotting brands.

>   **Source:** Hu, M., Qiu, P., Wan, F. & Stillman, T. (2018). Love or hate, depends on who's saying it: How legitimacy of brand rejection alters brand preferences. *Journal of Business Research, 90*, 164-170.

Brand relationship

Definition: Brand relationships suggests that individuals and brands can establish relationships with each other.

>   **Source:** Nyadzayo, M. W., Matanda, M. J. & Ewing, M. T. (2016). Franchisee-based brand equity: The role of brand relationship quality and brand citizenship behavior. *Industrial Marketing Management, 52*, 163-174.

Brand relationship quality

Definition: Brand relationship quality is defined as a customer's perceptions of how well the relationship fulfils the expectations, predictions, goals, and desires the customer has concerning the relationship.

>   **Source:** So Kevin Kam, F., King, C., Sparks Beverley, A. & Wang, Y. (2016). Enhancing customer relationships with retail service brands: the role of customer engagement. *Journal of Service Management, 27*(2).

Brand relationship quality

Definition (1): Brand relationship quality is proposed as a customer-based indicator of the relationship strength between a customer and brand.

> **Source:** Nyadzayo, M. W., Matanda, M. J. & Ewing, M. T. (2016). Franchisee-based brand equity: The role of brand relationship quality and brand citizenship behavior. *Industrial Marketing Management*, 52, 163-174.

Definition (2): Brand relationship quality is a higher-order construct composed of brand trust and brand commitment.

> **Source:** Nyadzayo, M. W., Matanda, M. J. & Ewing, M. T. (2016). Franchisee-based brand equity: The role of brand relationship quality and brand citizenship behavior. *Industrial Marketing Management*, 52, 163-174.

Brand relationship strength

Definition: Brand relationship strength is the level of commitment a consumer has to a brand and is determined by the combination of brand satisfaction and brand trust the consumer has for the brand.

> **Source:** Hayes, J. L., Golan, G., Britt, B. & Applequist, J. (2020). How advertising relevance and consumer–Brand relationship strength limit disclosure effects of native ads on Twitter. *International Journal of Advertising*, 39(1), 131-165.

Brand religiosity

Definition: Brand religiosity is the highest level that can be reached by a brand. Brand religion comes from the highest value that has highest product involvement, besides emotional values and rational values offered by the brand.

> **Source:** Wahyuni, S. & Fitriani, N. (2017). Brand religiosity aura and brand loyalty in Indonesia Islamic banking. *Journal of Islamic Marketing*, 8(3), 361-372.

Brand reputation

Definition (1): Brand reputation derives from the perspective of external stakeholders or wider audiences and is an aggregate set of public judgments whose valence may change over time.

> **Source:** Black, I. & Veloutsou, C. (2017). Working consumers: Co-creation of brand identity, consumer identity and brand community identity. *Journal of Business Research*, 70, 416-429.

Definition (2): Brand reputation is a perceptual representation of a company's past actions and future prospects that describes the brand's overall appeal to all of its key constituents when compared with other leading rivals.

> **Source:** Foroudi, P. (2019). Influence of brand signature, brand awareness, brand attitude, brand reputation on hotel industry's brand performance. *International Journal of Hospitality Management*, 76, 271-285.

Definition (3): Brand reputation refers to value judgments made about a brand's qualities, reliability and reliability and tends to be more durable than its image since it cannot be developed or changed quickly

> **Source:** Napoli, J., Dickinson-Delaporte, S. & Beverland, M. B. (2016). The brand authenticity continuum: strategic approaches for building value. *Journal of Marketing Management, 32*(13-14), 1201-1229.

Brand resonance

Definition (1): Brand resonance is the last element of the six building blocks (i.e. salience, performance, imagery, judgement, feelings and resonance) to construct Keller's brand equity.

> **Source:** Nyadzayo, M. W., Leckie, C. & Johnson, L. W. (2020). The impact of relational drivers on customer brand engagement and brand outcomes. *Journal of Brand Management, 27*(5), 561-578.

Definition (2): Brand resonance, which is the ultimate summit in Keller's Customer Based Brand Equity, sits on the top of the brand equity pyramid is a multidimensional construct that includes loyalty and attachment.

> **Source:** Cheng, Y.-Y., Tung, W.-F., Yang, M.-H. & Chiang, C.-T. (2019). Linking relationship equity to brand resonance in a social networking brand community. *Electronic Commerce Research and Applications, 35*, 100849.

Definition (3): Brand resonance refers to the nature of heightened brand-centric relationships and is characterized by intense psychological attachment with a brand as well as active behavior directed toward the brand's benefit.

> **Source:** Badrinarayanan, V. & Becerra, E. P. (2019). Antecedents and consequences of shoppers' attitude toward branded store-within-stores: An exploratory framework. *Journal of Business Research, 105*, 189-200.

Brand respect

Definition: Brand respect is the level of familiarity and favourability of the brand among the consumers.

> **Source:** Trivedi, J. & Sama, R. (2020). The Effect of Influencer Marketing on Consumers' Brand Admiration and Online Purchase Intentions: An Emerging Market Perspective. *Journal of Internet Commerce, 19*(1), 103-124.

Brand responses

Definition: Brand responses are brand strategies that encompass two main categories: accommodative or defensive . This distinction is based on whether the brand does or does not acknowledge responsibility for the customers' complaint.

> Source: Johnen, M. & Schnittka, O. (2019). When pushing back is good: the effectiveness of brand responses to social media complaints. *Journal of the Academy of Marketing Science, 47*(5), 858-878.

Brand resurrection movement

Definition: Brand resurrection movement refers to the process initiated by consumers to bring a defunct brand back to life.

> Source: Davari, A., Iyer, P. & Guzmán, F. (2017). Determinants of brand resurrection movements: Why consumers want dead brands back? *European Journal of Marketing, 51*(11/12), 1896-1917.

Brand retailer

Definition: Brand retailer is defined as a store brand (e.g. Wal-Mart)

> Source: Londoño, J. C., Elms, J. & Davies, K. (2016). Conceptualising and measuring consumer-based brand–retailer–channel equity. *Journal of Retailing and Consumer Services, 29*, 70-81.

Brand revitalization

Definition: Brand revitalization refers to capturing lost brand equity through enterprises, returning to their roots, to reverse the recession trend and regain a competitive advantage.

> Source: Li, C., Cui, Z., Chen, J. & Zhou, N. (2019). Brand Revitalization of Heritage Enterprises for Cultural Sustainability in the Digital Era: A Case Study in China. *Sustainability, 11*, 1769.

Brand rivalry

Definition: Brand rivalry is related to attitude polarization which occurs when the individual conforms to the perceived extreme group norm (intragroup identification) but simultaneously tends to distance herself from a disliked outgroup norm (intergroup alienation).

> Source: Osuna Ramírez Sergio, A., Veloutsou, C. & Morgan-Thomas, A. (2019). I hate what you love: brand polarization and negativity towards brands as an opportunity for brand management. *Journal of Product & Brand Management, 28*(5), 614-632.

Brand romance

Definition: Brand romance refers to a state of emotional attachment, evoked in response to the brand as a stimulus that is characterized by positive affect towards the brand, high arousal caused by the brand and a tendency of the brand to dominate the consumer's cognition.

> Source: Mpinganjira, M. & Maduku, D. K. (2019). Ethics of mobile behavioral advertising: Antecedents and outcomes of perceived ethical value of advertised brands. *Journal of Business Research, 95*, 464-478.

Brand salience

Definition: Brand salience, defined as the strength of awareness of the brand for a given products cathegory.

> **Source:** Dabbous, A. & Barakat, K. A. (2020). Bridging the online offline gap: Assessing the impact of brands' social network content quality on brand awareness and purchase intention. *Journal of Retailing and Consumer Services*, 53, 101966.

Brand satisfaction

Definition: Brand satisfaction is an evaluative summary of direct consumption experience mostly judged by the difference between prior expectation and the actual performance perceived after consumption.

> **Source:** Han, H., Nguyen, H. N., Song, H., Chua, B.-L., Lee, S. & Kim, W. (2018). Drivers of brand loyalty in the chain coffee shop industry. *International Journal of Hospitality Management*, 72, 86-97.

Brand scandal

Definition: Brand scandals are defined as negative events related to the brand. There are two types of scandals: performance and product-related scandals and scandals related to the brand's ability to offer functional benefits, as in the case of defective products.

> **Source:** Guèvremont, A. & Grohmann, B. (2018). Does brand authenticity alleviate the effect of brand scandals? *Journal of Brand Management*, 25(4), 322-336.

Brand scarcity

Definition: Brand scarcity (rare brand) is defined as the extent to which consumers perceive that the brand's goods or service outlets are not widely available or accessible.

> **Source:** Moulard, J. G., Raggio, R. D. & Folse, J. A. G. (2016). Brand Authenticity: Testing the Antecedents and Outcomes of Brand Management's Passion for its Products. *Psychology & Marketing*, 33(6), 421-436.

Brand schemata

Definition: Brand schemata refers to the cognitive structures that represent one's current perception of or expectations about a given product or brand.

> **Source:** Carsana, L. & Jolibert, A. (2018). Influence of iconic, indexical cues, and brand schematicity on perceived authenticity dimensions of private-label brands. *Journal of Retailing and Consumer Services*, 40, 213-220.

Brand schematicity

Definition: Brand schematicity is an individual characteristic and it is defined as the use of the brand as a central node in memory organization and storage.

> Source: Carsana, L. & Jolibert, A. (2018). Influence of iconic, indexical cues, and brand schematicity on perceived authenticity dimensions of private-label brands. *Journal of Retailing and Consumer Services, 40*, 213-220.

Brand score

Definition: Brand score is a measure of brand importance calculated on text data, combining methods of social network and semantic analysis.

> Source: Fronzetti Colladon, A. (2018). The Semantic Brand Score. *Journal of Business Research, 88*, 150-160.

Brand self connection

Definition: Brand self connection refers to the extent to which a customer develops the feeling of being connected to other brand users.

> Source: An, J., Do, D. K. X., Ngo, L. V. & Quan, T. H. M. (2019). Turning brand credibility into positive word-of-mouth: integrating the signaling and social identity perspectives. *Journal of Brand Management, 26*(2), 157-175.

Brand self-relevance

Definition: Brand self-relevance is defined as the extent to which the brand is appraised by consumers as being meaningful and relevant to them, and, accordingly, to their concerns (e.g., goals, needs).

> Source: Schnebelen, S. & Bruhn, M. (2018). An appraisal framework of the determinants and consequences of brand happiness. *Psychology & Marketing, 35*(2), 101-119.

Brand sensitivity

Definition: Brand sensitivity is a psychological variable which influences the consumer's purchase decision and signifies the nature and intensity of a cognitive, emotional or symbolic relationship between consumers and brands.

> Source: Alhosseini Almodarresi Seyed, M. & Rasty, F. (2019). The moderating effect of emotion regulation on the relationship between risk aversion and brand sensitivity. *Journal of Product & Brand Management, 28*(1), 95-103.

Brand sentiment

Definition: Brand sentiment is described as the sentiment expressed by social media users toward brands in their User generated content. It describes whether users have positive, neutral or negative attitude toward brands when commenting or reviewing them.

> Source: Roma, P. & Aloini, D. (2019). How does brand-related user-generated content differ across social media? Evidence reloaded. *Journal of Business Research, 96*, 322-339.

Brand signature

Definition: Brand signature is an original, distinctive design based on the brand personality and identity that is carried across all brand communications. Brand signature refers to the endorsement of consistent consumer attitude toward diffusion of a brand name and brand logo (consists of typeface, design, and color), and the expression and pursuit of a distinct message and the quality of the organization.

> **Source:** Foroudi, P. (2019). Influence of brand signature, brand awareness, brand attitude, brand reputation on hotel industry's brand performance. *International Journal of Hospitality Management, 76*, 271-285.

Brand skills

Definition: Brand skills are defined as the extent to which consumers perceive their own performance as emanating from their use of a particular brand. Brand skill experiences are stored in memory, becoming a part of the associative network surrounding the brand.

> **Source:** Mohan, M., Jiménez Fernando, R., Brown Brian, P. & Cantrell, C. (2017). Brand skill: linking brand functionality with consumer-based brand equity. *Journal of Product & Brand Management, 26*(5), 477-491.

Brand skills

Definition: Brand skills represent the extent to which stakeholders are stimulated by the brand in terms of their capabilities.

> **Source:** Merz, M. A., Zarantonello, L. & Grappi, S. (2018). How valuable are your customers in the brand value co-creation process? The development of a Customer Co-Creation Value (CCCV) scale. *Journal of Business Research, 82*, 79-89.

Brand social networks narratives

Definition: Brand social networks narratives is defined as messages on social media that viewers (consumers) may interpret as being related to goods, services and experiences offered by luxury brands.

> **Source:** Huang, R., Ha, S. & Kim, S.-H. (2018). Narrative persuasion in social media: an empirical study of luxury brand advertising. *Journal of Research in Interactive Marketing, 12*(3), 274-292.

Brand social responsibility

Definition: Brand social responsibility refers to the extent to which consumers perceive that a brand and sustained voluntary activities associated with the brand improve the welfare of society.

> **Source:** Vuong, B. N. & Khanh Giao, H. N. (2020). The Impact of Perceived Brand Globalness on Consumers' Purchase Intention and the Moderating Role of Consumer

Ethnocentrism: An Evidence from Vietnam. *Journal of International Consumer Marketing, 32*(1), 47-68.

Brand social self-expressiveness

Definition: Brand social self-expressiveness is defined as a brand's ability to project one's desirable social image and is related to a consumer's private mental world.

Source: Sarkar, A., Sarkar, J. G., Sreejesh, S., Anusree, M. R. & Rishi, B. (2020). You are so embarrassing, still, I hate you less! Investigating consumers' brand embarrassment and brand hate. *Journal of Brand Management, 27*(1), 93-107.

Brand specific transformational leadership

Definition: Brand-specifc transformational leadership has been defned as a leader's approach to motivating his or her followers to act on behalf of the corporate brand, by appealing to their values and personal convictions.

Source: Chiang, H.-H., Han, T.-S. & C. McConville, D. (2020). A multilevel study of brand-specific transformational leadership: employee and customer effects. *Journal of Brand Management, 27*(3), 312-327.

Brand specific transactional leadership

Definition: Brand-specific transactional leadership is defined as a leader's approach to motivating followers to act on behalf of the corporate brand, by appealing to personal values and convictions.

Source: Punjaisri, K., Evanschitzky, H. & Rudd, J. (2013). Aligning employee service recovery performance with brand values: The role of brand-specific leadership. *Journal of Marketing Management, 29*(9-10), 981-1006.

Brand stability

Definition: Brand stability refers to brand consistent behaviors

Source: Moulard, J. G., Raggio, R. D. & Folse, J. A. G. (2016). Brand Authenticity: Testing the Antecedents and Outcomes of Brand Management's Passion for its Products. *Psychology & Marketing, 33*(6), 421-436.

Brand status

Definition: Brand status is defined as the prestige of a brand or where a brand stands in consumers' minds relative to other brands and is an important part of brand equity.

Source: Hu, M., Qiu, P., Wan, F. & Stillman, T. (2018). Love or hate, depends on who's saying it: How legitimacy of brand rejection alters brand preferences. *Journal of Business Research, 90*, 164-170.

Brand stereotype

Definition: Brand stereotype is essentially a commonly held set of beliefs or impressions about the characteristics of members belonging to a particular brand or brand community.

>**Source:** Davvetas, V. & Halkias, G. (2019). Global and local brand stereotypes: formation, content transfer, and impact. *International Marketing Review, 36*(5), 675-701.

Brand story

Definition (1): Brand story is a temporal sequence of events, and convey actions of characters and it is structured around a coherent theme and is an effective means of brand communication because they elicit emotions.

>**Source:** Nguyen, T.-T. & Grohmann, B. (2020). The influence of passion/determination and external disadvantage on consumer responses to brand biographies. *Journal of Brand Management, 27*(4), 452-465.

Definition (2): Brand story consists of brand events that are carried out by actors.

>**Source:** Solja, E., Liljander, V. & Söderlund, M. (2018). Short brand stories on packaging: An examination of consumer responses. *Psychology & Marketing, 35*(4), 294-306.

Brand story transportation

Definition: Brand transportation is an intensive form of absorption and is defined as a distinct mental process where the consumer is carried away by the story to the degree that she or he is "lost" in it.

>**Source:** Solja, E., Liljander, V. & Söderlund, M. (2018). Short brand stories on packaging: An examination of consumer responses. *Psychology & Marketing, 35*(4), 294-306.

Brand storytelling

Definition: Brand storytelling applies personified narratives to portray historical events and involves explaining the product design, the origin of the brand and any memorable events during the relationship between consumers and brands.

>**Source:** Kao Danny, T. & Wu, P.-H. (2019). The impact of affective orientation on bank preference as moderated by cognitive load and brand story style. *International Journal of Bank Marketing, 37*(5), 1334-1349.

Brand strength

Definition: Brand strength embodies the weight consumer grants to a brand as an informational criterion in the process that precedes the buying act.

Source: Korai, B. (2017). Determinants of African Women's Brand Sensitivity Toward Cosmetics. *Journal of International Consumer Marketing, 29*(4), 250-264.

Brand success

Definition: Brand success is associated to a high performance in brand indicators (e.g., market share and market penetration, purchasing per buyer).

Source: Molinillo, S., Ekinci, Y. & Japutra, A. (2019). A consumer-based brand performance model for assessing brand success. *International Journal of Market Research, 61*(1), 93-110.

Brand superiority

Definition: Brand superiority is defined as the extent to which customer views the brand to be unique or better than other brands, and is the result of individuals' judgments of brands and their meanings.

Source: Davari, A., Iyer, P. & Guzmán, F. (2017). Determinants of brand resurrection movements: Why consumers want dead brands back? *European Journal of Marketing, 51*(11/12), 1896-1917.

Brand supportive intentions

Definition: Brand supportive intentions is defined as post-purchase/consumption behaviors that the consumer intends to take to benefit the brand, such as repeat purchasing and recommending the brand to others.

Source: Wu, H.-C. & Chang, Y.-Y. (2019). What drives brand supportive intentions? *Marketing Intelligence & Planning, 37*(5), 497-512.

Brand surfeits

Definition: Brand surfeits. is generated around the brand by social media practices such as discussion forums, blogs, social platforms and video, photo and news-sharing sites. Brand surfeits are material forms and immateria.

Source: Cova, B. & Paranque, B. (2016). Value slippage in brand transformation: a conceptualization. *Journal of Product & Brand Management, 25*(1), 3-10.

Brand sustainability

Definition: Brand sustainability is viewed as a brand which is having high brand value creates a sustainable competitive advantage which leads to brand sustainability.

Source: Ray, K. & Sharma, M. (2020). Antecedents and Outcomes of Brand Strength: A Study of Asian IT Organizations Towards Brand Sustainability. *Corporate Reputation Review*.

Brand symbolism

Definition: Brand symbolism understanding has previously been operationalised as a user's ability to make judgments about the ways in which brands are used.

> **Source:** Watkins, L., Aitken, R., Thyne, M., Robertson, K. & Borzekowski, D. (2017). Environmental influences on pre-schooler's understanding of brand symbolism. *Marketing Intelligence & Planning*, 35(7), 907-922.

Brand synonymity

Definition: Brand synonymity is defined as 'a prime leadership position a brand reaches, when the brand name becomes a word (as a noun, verb or adjective) in the consumer vocabulary.

> **Source:** Kumar, S. M. & Jayasimha, K. R. (2019). Brand verbs: brand synonymity and brand leadership. *Journal of Brand Management*, 26(2), 110-125.

Brand tarnishment

Definition: Brand tarnishment is the detriment to repute or trademark tarnishment when a mark is 'sullied or debased by its associations with something inappropriate' either through use in an unpleasant, obscene, or degrading context, or in a context that is not acceptable.

> **Source:** Boshoff, C. (2016). The lady doth protest too much: a neurophysiological perspective on brand tarnishment. *Journal of Product & Brand Management*, 25(2), 196-207.

Brand transformation

Definition: Brand transformation is a multidimensional construct with 4 dimensions: Brand appropriation; Brand genericization. ; Brand surfeiting; Brand regeneration.

> **Source:** Cova, B. & Paranque, B. (2016). Value slippage in brand transformation: a conceptualization. *Journal of Product & Brand Management*, 25(1), 3-10.

Brand transgression

Definition: Brand transgression is defined as brand actions that could allow the incorporation of a large array of negative events (e.g., service failures and product-harm crises).

> **Source:** Khamitov, M., Grégoire, Y. & Suri, A. (2020). A systematic review of brand transgression, service failure recovery and product-harm crisis: integration and guiding insights. *Journal of the Academy of Marketing Science*, 48(3), 519-542.

Brand tribalism

Definition: Brand tribes are associated with the individuals that bound together through shared interpersonal and social experiences.

> Source: Taute Harry, A., Sierra Jeremy, J., Carter Larry, L. & Maher Amro, A. (2017). A sequential process of brand tribalism, brand pride and brand attitude to explain purchase intention: a cross-continent replication study. *Journal of Product & Brand Management, 26*(3), 239-250.

Brand tribe

Definition: Brand tribe refers to the members of a brand tribe that are fixed in a hearty emotional bond to such an entity or brand whether product or brand. Brand tribes are differentiated from brand communities in that tribes do not control consumers' lives.

> Source: Taute Harry, A., Sierra Jeremy, J., Carter Larry, L. & Maher Amro, A. (2017). A sequential process of brand tribalism, brand pride and brand attitude to explain purchase intention: a cross-continent replication study. *Journal of Product & Brand Management, 26*(3), 239-250.

Brand trust

Definition (1): Brand trust refers to the extent to which a stakeholder is confident about the brand and it is the tendency of the customer to believe that a brand keeps its promises.

> Source: Merz, M. A., Zarantonello, L. & Grappi, S. (2018). How valuable are your customers in the brand value co-creation process? The development of a Customer Co-Creation Value (CCCV) scale. *Journal of Business Research, 82*, 79-89.

Definition (2): Brand trust is defined as the confident expectations of the brand's reliability and intentions in situations entailing risk to the consumer.

> Source: Roy, V., Tata, S. V. & Parsad, C. (2018). Consumer response to brand involved in food safety scandal: An exploratory study based on a recent scandal in India. *Journal of Consumer Behaviour, 17*(1), 25-33.

Definition (3): Brand trust is defined as a willingness to rely on an exchange partner in whom one has confidence.

> Source: So Kevin Kam, F., King, C., Sparks Beverley, A. & Wang, Y. (2016). Enhancing customer relationships with retail service brands: the role of customer engagement. *Journal of Service Management, 27*(2).

Definition (4): Brand trust is defined as the willingness of the average customer to rely on the brand's ability to perform its function.

> Source: Molinillo, S., Japutra, A., Nguyen, B. & Chen Cheng-Hao, S. (2017). Responsible brands vs active brands? An examination of brand personality on brand awareness, brand trust, and brand loyalty. *Marketing Intelligence & Planning, 35*(2), 166-179.

Definition (5): Brand trust is a consumer's certainty of expected positive consequences when purchasing the product of a particular brand.

> **Source:** Chen-Yu, J., Cho, S. & Kincade, D. (2016). Brand perception and brand repurchase intent in online apparel shopping: An examination of brand experience, image congruence, brand affect, and brand trust. *Journal of Global Fashion Marketing, 7*(1), 30-44.

Definition (6): Brand trust relates to a consumer's belief that a brand will perform as expected or promised, and a firm will endeavour to resolve any problems or issues that may arise.

> **Source:** Napoli, J., Dickinson-Delaporte, S. & Beverland, M. B. (2016). The brand authenticity continuum: strategic approaches for building value. *Journal of Marketing Management, 32*(13-14), 1201-1229.

Definition (7): Brand trust refers to consumers' confidence that the brand, product, or service firm is dependable and competent.

> **Source:** Lude, M. & Prügl, R. (2018). Why the family business brand matters: Brand authenticity and the family firm trust inference. *Journal of Business Research, 89*, 121-134.

Definition (8): Brand trust is a customer's willingness to rely on the ability of the brand to perform its stated function, especially in uncertain situations.

> **Source:** Nyadzayo, M. W., Leckie, C. & Johnson, L. W. (2020). The impact of relational drivers on customer brand engagement and brand outcomes. *Journal of Brand Management, 27*(5), 561-578.

Brand trustworthiness

Definition: Brand trustworthiness denotes consumers' perceptions of the willingness of the brand to keep and deliver its promises.

> **Source:** Zhang, B., Ritchie, B., Mair, J. & Driml, S. (2019). Is the Airline Trustworthy? The Impact of Source Credibility on Voluntary Carbon Offsetting. *Journal of Travel Research, 58*(5), 715-731.

Brand truth

Definition (1): Brand truth is defined as the original intention of the brand custodians which reflects accurately the qualities and reality of the brand promise, and how this truth is to be packaged to reflect the different settings, channels, and pressures on the brand.

> **Source:** Karanges, E., Johnston, K. A., Lings, I. & Beatson, A. T. (2018). Brand signalling: An antecedent of employee brand understanding. *Journal of Brand Management, 25*(3), 235-249.

Definition (2): Brand truth refers to the original intention of the brand custodians which reflects accurately the qualities and reality of the brand promise.

> Source: Karanges, E., Johnston, K. A., Lings, I. & Beatson, A. T. (2018). Brand signalling An antecedent of employee brand understanding. *Journal of Brand Management* 25(3), 235-249.

Brand understanding

Definition: Brand understanding is defined as individuals' comprehension of brand-related information.

> Source: Karanges, E., Johnston, K. A., Lings, I. & Beatson, A. T. (2018). Brand signalling An antecedent of employee brand understanding. *Journal of Brand Management* 25(3), 235-249.

Brand uniqueness

Definition: Brand uniqueness refers to the extent to which a consumer regards the brand as different from other brands.

> Source: Southworth Sarah, S. & Ha-Brookshire, J. (2016). The impact of cultural authenticity on brand uniqueness and willingness to try: The case of Chinese brands and US consumers. *Asia Pacific Journal of Marketing and Logistics*, 28(4), 724-742.

Brand value

Definition: Brand value is the customers' perceived balance between a product's price and utility and it is as the strategic outcome of marketing initiatives of a firm useful to measure the effectiveness of efficiency of other organisational strategies.

> Source: Gupta, S., Gallear, D., Rudd, J. & Foroudi, P. (2020). The impact of brand value on brand competitiveness. *Journal of Business Research*, 112, 210-222.

Brand values

Definition (1): Brand values refers to the overarching concepts that summarize brand identity and serve as guiding principles for the brand building process.

> Source: Taks, M., Seguin, B., Naraine, M. L., Thompson, A., Parent, M. M. & Hoye, R. (2020). Brand governance practices in Canadian national sport organizations: an exploratory study. *European Sport Management Quarterly*, 20(1), 10-29.

Definition (2): Brand values is the desirable goals, varying in importance, that serve as guiding principles in brands' lives.

Source: Swoboda, B., Puchert, C. & Morschett, D. (2016). Explaining the differing effects of corporate reputation across nations: a multilevel analysis. *Journal of the Academy of Marketing Science, 44*(4), 454-473.

Brand variant

Definition: Brand variant is defined as the different SKU (stock keeping unit) that a brand makes available to its consumers (e.g., size, flavor, ingredients).

Source: Hökelekli, G., Lamey, L. & Verboven, F. (2017). Private label line proliferation and private label tier pricing: A new dimension of competition between private labels and national brands. *Journal of Retailing and Consumer Services, 36*, 39-52.

Brand vision

Definition: The vision of the brand is a definition of the purpose and objective of the brand in the long term.

Source: Bridson, K. C. & Evans, J. (2018). Brand compass: charting a course to improve firm performance. *Journal of Strategic Marketing, 26*(2), 174-187.

Brand work

Definition: Brand work refers to the perceived effort of the brand (i.e., its determination). brand work is a construct that is related to consumer perceptions of the extent to which the brand tries hard, puts in effort, and is hard-working.

Source: Baxter, S. M. & Ilicic, J. (2018). May the force drag your dynamic logo: The brand work-energy effect. *International Journal of Research in Marketing, 35*(3), 509-523.

Branded community

Definition: Branded community is defined as the individuals that revolve around any interest or need (not a brand).

Source: Popp, B. & Woratschek, H. (2016). Introducing branded communities in sport for building strong brand relations in social media. *Sport Management Review, 19*(2), 183-197.

Branded emoticon

Definition: Branded emoticons refer to emoticons with a brand logo, brand mascot, brand avatar or brand-related information.

Source: Lee Crystal, T. & Hsieh Sara, H. (2019). Engaging consumers in mobile instant messaging: the role of cute branded emoticons. *Journal of Product & Brand Management, 28*(7), 849-863.

Branded merchandise

Definition: Brand merchandise represents a form of niche speciality store that offer a selection of licensed products, décor, and gift/novelty items.

>Source: Hyllegard, K. H., Ogle, J. P., Yan, R.-N. & Kissell, K. (2016). Consumer response to exterior atmospherics at a university-branded merchandise store. *Fashion and Textiles*, 3(1), 4.

Branding

Definition: Branding is defined as the use of brand elements (e.g., name, term, design, symbol, or other feature).

>Source: Zhang, J., Jiang, Y., Shabbir, R. & Zhu, M. (2016). How brand orientation impacts B2B service brand equity? An empirical study among Chinese firms. *Journal of Business & Industrial Marketing*, 31(1), 83-98.

Brand-post congruence

Definition: Brand-post congruence refers to the extent to which the brand's posts (in Social networks) are conform to consumers' expectations and perceptions of what may be relevant to the brand, based on their activated schema.

>Source: Wang, S. S., Lin, Y.-C. & Liang, T.-P. (2018). Posts that attract millions of fans: The effect of brand-post congruence. *Electronic Commerce Research and Applications*, 28, 73-85.

Brand–Retailer–Channel Awareness

Definition: Brand–Retailer–Channel Associations is defined as the ability to recognise or recall a brand sold in certain retailer as part or member of a specific environment or channel.

>Source: Londoño, J. C., Elms, J. & Davies, K. (2016). Conceptualising and measuring consumer-based brand–retailer–channel equity. *Journal of Retailing and Consumer Services*, 29, 70-81.

Brand–Retailer–Channel Consumer Loyalty

Definition: Brand–retailer–channel Consumer Loyalty is defined as consumers' deeply held commitment to re-buy or re-patronise a preferred brand–retailer–channel consistently in the future.

>Source: Londoño, J. C., Elms, J. & Davies, K. (2016). Conceptualising and measuring consumer-based brand–retailer–channel equity. *Journal of Retailing and Consumer Services*, 29, 70-81.

Brand-retailer-channel perceived quality

Definition: Brand-retailer-channel perceived quality is defined as the perception of the overall quality or superiority of a brand-retailer-channel with respect to its intended purpose relative to alternatives.

> **Source:** Londoño, J. C., Elms, J. & Davies, K. (2016). Conceptualising and measuring consumer-based brand-retailer-channel equity. *Journal of Retailing and Consumer Services*, 29, 70-81.

Business performance

Definition: Business performance relates to value creation, enhancement, and dissemination to customers.

> **Source:** Garg, P., Gupta, B., Dzever, S., Sivarajah, U. & Kumar, V. (2020). Examining the Relationship between Social Media Analytics Practices and Business Performance in the Indian Retail and IT Industries: The Mediation Role of Customer Engagement. *International Journal of Information Management*, 52, 102069.

Cause related marketing

Definition: Cause related marketing is defined as the process of formulating and implementing the marketing activities that are characterized by an offer from the firm to contribute a specified amount of money to a chosen cause.

> **Source:** Ullah, S., Lei, S., Qureshi, S. & Haider, J. (2017). Selecting the Right Cause from the Right Category: Does the Role of Product Category Matter in Cause-Brand Alliance? A Case Study of Students in Shanghai Universities. *Iranian Journal of Management Studies*, 10, 365-383.

Cause-brand alliance

Definition: Cause-brand alliance is a partnership between causes and brands

> **Source:** Vahdati, Y. & Voss Kevin, E. (2019). Brand identification, cause-brand alliances and perceived cause controversy. *Journal of Product & Brand Management*, 28(7), 880-892.

CBBE (customer based brand equity)

Definition: Keller proposed a CBBE pyramid model that involves four ladders, namely, brand identity, brand meaning, brand response, and brand relationship and six brand building sections, namely, brand salience, brand performance, brand imagery, brand judgements, brand feelings, and brand resonance.

> **Source:** Cheng, Y.-Y., Tung, W.-F., Yang, M.-H. & Chiang, C.-T. (2019). Linking relationship equity to brand resonance in a social networking brand community. *Electronic Commerce Research and Applications*, 35, 100849.

CBRs constructs (Customer Brand relationships constructs)
Definition: Customer brand relationships constructs are brand awareness, brand trust, and brand loyalty.

> **Source:** Molinillo, S., Japutra, A., Nguyen, B. & Chen Cheng-Hao, S. (2017). Responsible brands vs active brands? An examination of brand personality on brand awareness, brand trust, and brand loyalty. *Marketing Intelligence & Planning*, 35(2), 166-179.

Celebrity
Definition: A celebrity is defined as a widely-known personality who is recognized by a certain group of people. They have some characteristics, such as attractiveness, extraordinary lifestyle, or special skills. Celebrities are considered as credible sources of information and motivated.

> **Source:** Min, J. H. J., Chang, H. J. J., Jai, T.-M. C. & Ziegler, M. (2019). The effects of celebrity-brand congruence and publicity on consumer attitudes and buying behavior. *Fashion and Textiles*, 6(1), 10.

Celebrity credibility
Definition: Celebrity credibility is defined as the extent to which the recipient perceives the source as having relevant knowledge and/or experience, and therefore, trusts the source to give unbiased information.

> **Source:** Cuomo, M., Foroudi, P., Tortora, D., Hussain, S. & Melewar, T. C. (2019). Celebrity Endorsement and the Attitude Towards Luxury Brands for Sustainable Consumption. *Sustainability*, 11, 6791.

Celbrity endorser
Definition: Celebrity endorser is any individual who enjoys public recognition and who uses this recognition on behalf of a consumer good by appearing with it in an advertisement.

> **Source:** Kang, J. & Choi, W. J. (2016). Endorsed Sustainable Products:The Role of Celebrity Ethicality and Brand Ethicality. *Clothing and Textiles Research Journal*, 34(4), 303-319.

Celebrity endorsements
Definition: Celebrity endorsements refer to a form of advertising strategy in which a famous or well-known person uses her or his social status to promote a good, service, or idea. Celebrity status can arise from a person's talent and skill in a particular area.

> **Source:** Winterich, K. P., Gangwar, M. & Grewal, R. (2018). When Celebrities Count: Power Distance Beliefs and Celebrity Endorsements. *Journal of Marketing*, 82(3), 70-86.

Celebrity image

Definition: Celebrity image is the consumers' perception about an individual who enjoys massive popularity among the masses, which is revealed by the celebrity associations existing in the consumers' minds.

> **Source:** Mann, B. J. S., Parmar, Y. & Ghuman, M. K. (2020) A New Scale to Capture the Multidimensionality of Celebrity Image. *Global Business Review*, *0*(0), 0972150920919599.

Channel equity

Definition: Channel equity can be defined 'as the net present value of the current and future profits generated through a distribution channel (Consumer-Based Brand–Retailer–Channel).

> **Source:** Londoño, J. C., Elms, J. & Davies, K. (2016). Conceptualising and measuring consumer-based brand–retailer–channel equity. *Journal of Retailing and Consumer Services*, *29*, 70-81.

Chatbots

Definition: Chatbots is defined as interactive messaging powered by artifitial intellingence. Aditionally, chatbots is a service, powered by rules and sometimes artificial intelligence that you interact with via a chat interface.

> **Source:** Trivedi, J. (2019). Examining the Customer Experience of Using Banking Chatbots and Its Impact on Brand Love: The Moderating Role of Perceived Risk. *Journal of Internet Commerce*, *18*(1), 91-111.

City attachment

Definition: City attachment is multidisciplinary and is defined as the emotional bond between an individual and a particular place/city. It is a an individual's cognitive or emotional connection to a particular setting.

> **Source:** Yu & Kim. (2020). The Relationship between Self-City Brand Connection, City Brand Experience, and City Brand Ambassadors. *Sustainability*, *12*, 982.

City brand ambassadorship behavior

Definition: City brand ambassadorship behavior can be defined as sharing positive experiences about the residents' city through word-of-mouth and advocating for it.

> **Source:** Yu & Kim. (2020). The Relationship between Self-City Brand Connection, City Brand Experience, and City Brand Ambassadors. *Sustainability*, *12*, 982.

City brand experience

Definition: City brand experience is expressed by the interaction between the consumer and the city brand.

Source: Yu & Kim. (2020). The Relationship between Self-City Brand Connection, City Brand Experience, and City Brand Ambassadors. *Sustainability*, *12*, 982.

Co-branding

Definition (1): Co-branding is a brand alliance strategy in which two or more brands collaborate and launch their co-brand.

Source: Shen, B., Choi, T.-M. & Chow, P.-S. (2017). Brand loyalties in designer luxury and fast fashion co-branding alliances. *Journal of Business Research*, *81*, 173-180.

Definition (2): Co-branding is defined as a form of cooperation between two or more brands with a branding strategy which is popular in consumer products that pairs two or more branded products to form a separate and unique product.

Source: Londoño, J. C., Elms, J. & Davies, K. (2016). Conceptualising and measuring consumer-based brand–retailer–channel equity. *Journal of Retailing and Consumer Services*, *29*, 70-81.

Co-creation

Definition: Co-creation is an active, creative and social process based on collaboration between producers and consumers.

Source: Wu, H.-C. & Chang, Y.-Y. (2019). What drives brand supportive intentions? *Marketing Intelligence & Planning*, *37*(5), 497-512.

Cognition

Definition: Cognition is defined as the mental process of knowing, including aspects such as awareness, perception, reasoning, and judgment, which comes to be known, as through perception, reasoning, or intuition.

Source: Han, H., Nguyen, H. N., Song, H., Chua, B.-L., Lee, S. & Kim, W. (2018). Drivers of brand loyalty in the chain coffee shop industry. *International Journal of Hospitality Management*, *72*, 86-97.

Cognitive brand trust

Definition: Cognitive brand trust is defined as knowledge-driven trust in a brand, where faith is developed on the basis of good reasons for which brand is chosen.

Source: Srivastava, N., Dash Satya, B. & Mookerjee, A. (2015). Antecedents and moderators of brand trust in the context of baby care toiletries. *Journal of Consumer Marketing*, *32*(5), 328-340.

Cognitive load
Definition: Cognitive load is usually regarded as a multi-faceted complex construct, which consists of mental load and mental effort related to a brand.

>Source: Kao Danny, T. & Wu, P.-H. (2019). The impact of affective orientation on bank preference as moderated by cognitive load and brand story style. *International Journal of Bank Marketing*, 37(5), 1334-1349.

Cognitive loyalty
Definition: Cognitive loyalty refers to opinions and beliefs of individuals towards products, stores or brands which is influenced by information which is available about the product brand.

>Source: Nikhashemi, S. R. & Valaei, N. (2018). The chain of effects from brand personality and functional congruity to stages of brand loyalty: The moderating role of gender. *Asia Pacific Journal of Marketing and Logistics*, 30(1), 84-105.

Cognitive manifestations of brand fidelity
Definition: Cognitive manifestations of brand fidelity refers to the degree to which an individual feels "at one" with the brand partner and takes personal ownership of the brand.

>Source: Grace, D., Ross, M. & King, C. (2018). Brand fidelity: a relationship maintenance perspective. *Journal of Brand Management*, 25(6), 577-590.

Cognitive processing
Definition (1): Cognitive processing refers to a consumer's level of brand-related thought processing and elaboration in a particular consumer/brand interaction and also relates to a set of enduring and active mental states that a customer experiences.

>Source: Duong, G. H., Wu, W.-Y. & Le, L. H. (2020). The effects of brand page characteristics on customer brand engagement: moderating roles of community involvement and comedy production contents. *Journal of Brand Management*, 27(5), 531-545.

Commercial sponsorship
Definition: Commercial sponsorship refers to the sponsorship of various commercial activities (e.g. related to sports, arts) and has the objective to gain direct commercial benefits associated with brand awareness, image, and sales.

>Source: Shin, H., Lee, H. & Perdue, R. R. (2018). The congruity effects of commercial brand sponsorship in a regional event. *Tourism Management*, 67, 168-179.

Commitment
Definition (1): Commitment is the extent to which the stakeholder is willing to work for the brand and its success.

> Source: Merz, M. A., Zarantonello, L. & Grappi, S. (2018). How valuable are your customers in the brand value co-creation process? The development of a Customer Co-Creation Value (CCCV) scale. *Journal of Business Research, 82*, 79-89.

Definition (2): Commitment defines as an enduring desire to continue the relationship in conjunction with the willingness to make efforts toward that end.

> Source: Jeon Jung, O. & Baeck, S. (2016). What drives consumer's responses to brand crisis? The moderating roles of brand associations and brand-customer relationship strength. *Journal of Product & Brand Management, 25*(6), 550-567.

Community citizenship behaviour

Definition: Community citizenship behaviour can be considered as a direct extra-role behaviour and is defined as the voluntary and discretionary behaviour that directly promotes the effective function.

> Source: Wong, T. C., Haddoud Mohamed, Y., Kwok, Y. K. & He, H. (2018). Examining the key determinants towards online pro-brand and anti-brand community citizenship behaviours: A two-stage approach. *Industrial Management & Data Systems, 118*(4), 850-872

Community identification

Definition: Community identification is defined as a perceived emotionally connected membership to a certain online community.

> Source: Chang, Y., Hou, R.-J., Wang, K., Cui, A. P. & Zhang, C.-B. (2020). Effects of intrinsic and extrinsic motivation on social loafing in online travel communities. *Computers in Human Behavior, 109*, 106360.

Compatibility

Definition: Compatibility is defined as the degree to which the product (or brand) is perceived to be consistent with one's existing wardrobe and appropriateness for one's current needs and lifestyle.

> Source: Hwang, C. & Kim, T. H. (2020) Muslim Women's Purchasing Behaviors Toward Modest Activewear in the United States. *Clothing and Textiles Research Journal, 0*(0), 0887302X20926573.

Complaint

Definition: Complaint refers to a behavioral expression of dissatisfaction for the purpose of venting emotions or achieving intrapsychic goals, interpersonal goals, or both" (e.g., feeling relief, receiving compensation, or social positioning).

> Source: Johnen, M. & Schnittka, O. (2019). When pushing back is good: the effectiveness of brand responses to social media complaints. *Journal of the Academy of Marketing Science, 47*(5), 858-878.

Conative brand loyalty
Definition: Conative loyalty is associated with future behavioural intention towards the product brand.

>**Source:** Nikhashemi, S. R. & Valaei, N. (2018). The chain of effects from brand personality and functional congruity to stages of brand loyalty: The moderating role of gender. *Asia Pacific Journal of Marketing and Logistics, 30*(1), 84-105.

Congruency
Definition: Congruency is perceived when the brand displays a deep commitment to its values by ensuring that those values are reflected in its actions.

>**Source:** Portal, S., Abratt, R. & Bendixen, M. (2018). Building a human brand: Brand anthropomorphism unravelled. *Business Horizons, 61*(3), 367-374.

Congruity
Definition: Congruity is defined as the perception of fit between objects; humans evaluate different objects and develop attitudes based on the perceived congruity between them.

>**Source:** Shin, H., Lee, H. & Perdue, R. R. (2018). The congruity effects of commercial brand sponsorship in a regional event. *Tourism Management, 67*, 168-179.

Connectedness
Definition: Connectedness refers to customers' interpersonal ties within a brand social network.

>**Source:** Merz, M. A., Zarantonello, L. & Grappi, S. (2018). How valuable are your customers in the brand value co-creation process? The development of a Customer Co-Creation Value (CCCV) scale. *Journal of Business Research, 82*, 79-89.

Conscientiousness
Definition: Conscientiousness is related to the people that are organized, reliable, hard-working, self-disciplined, punctual, scrupulous, neat, ambitious, and persevering.

>**Source:** Vashist, D. (2018). Effect of product involvement and brand prominence on advergamers' brand recall and brand attitude in an emerging market context. *Asia Pacific Journal of Marketing and Logistics, 30*(1), 43-61.

Consumer empowerment
Definition: Consumer empowerment can be defined as giving consumers power through resources such as greater information or understanding.

> Source: Wu, H.-C. & Chang, Y.-Y. (2019). What drives brand supportive intentions? *Marketing Intelligence & Planning, 37*(5), 497-512.

Consumer ethnocentrism

Definition: Consumer ethnocentrism can be viewed as the beliefs held by consumers about the appropriateness, indeed morality, of purchasing foreign-made products.

> Source: Vuong, B. N. & Khanh Giao, H. N. (2020). The Impact of Perceived Brand Globalness on Consumers' Purchase Intention and the Moderating Role of Consumer Ethnocentrism: An Evidence from Vietnam. *Journal of International Consumer Marketing, 32*(1),

Consumer online engagement level

Definition: Consumer online engagement represents the interaction and participation of individuals within the social media environment. This includes reacting to content such as liking, commenting, and sharing.

> Source: Dabbous, A. & Barakat, K. A. (2020). Bridging the online offline gap: Assessing the impact of brands' social network content quality on brand awareness and purchase intention. *Journal of Retailing and Consumer Services, 53*, 101966.

Consumer persuasion knowledge

Definition: Consumer persuasion knowledge is defined as the knowledge that enables consumers to recognize, analyze, interpret, evaluate and remember persuasion attempts and to select and execute coping tactics believed to be effective and appropriate.

> Source: Vashisht, D. & Royne, M. B. (2016). Advergame speed influence and brand recall: The moderating effects of brand placement strength and gamers' persuasion knowledge. *Computers in Human Behavior, 63*, 162-169.

Consumer vanity

Definition: Consumer vanity is defined as an excessive concern for and/or a positive (perhaps inflated) view of one's physical appearance.

> Source: Sharda, N. & Bhat, A. (2019). Role of consumer vanity and the mediating effect of brand consciousness in luxury consumption. *Journal of Product & Brand Management, 28*(7), 800-811.

Consumer-brand engagement

Definition: Consumer-brand engagement (in a Social Media context) is defined as a consumer's positively valenced brand-related cognitive, emotional and behavioral activity during or related to focal consumer/brand interaction.

Source: Bazi, S., Filieri, R. & Gorton, M. (2020). Customers' motivation to engage with luxury brands on social media. *Journal of Business Research*, *112*, 223-235.

Consumer-brand identification

Definition (1): Consumer-brand identification can be defined as consumer's perceived state of oneness with a brand.

Source: Sichtmann, C., Davvetas, V. & Diamantopoulos, A. (2019). The relational value of perceived brand globalness and localness. *Journal of Business Research*, *104*, 597-613.

Definition (2): Consumer-brand identification is related to the primary psychological substrate for that kind of deep, committed, and meaningful relationships that marketers are increasingly seeking to build with their customers.

Source: Elbedweihy, A. M., Jayawardhena, C., Elsharnouby, M. H. & Elsharnouby, T. H. (2016). Customer relationship building: The role of brand attractiveness and consumer–brand identification. *Journal of Business Research*, *69*(8), 2901-2910.

Consumer-perceived brand authenticity

Definition: Consumer-perceived brand authenticity is the extent to which consumers perceive a brand to be faithful toward itself (continuity), true to its consumers (credibility), motivated by caring and responsibility (integrity), and able to support consumers in being true to themselves (symbolism).

Source: Charlton, A. B. & Cornwell, T. B. (2019). Authenticity in horizontal marketing partnerships: A better measure of brand compatibility. *Journal of Business Research*, *100*, 279-298.

Consumers brand credibility

Definition: Consumers brand credibility refers to the believability of the product information contained in a product.

Source: Kim, K., Choi, H.-j. & Hyun, S. (2020). Coffee House Consumers' Value Perception and Its Consequences: Multi-Dimensional Approach. *Sustainability*, *12*, 1663.

Consumers' brand evaluations

Definition: Consumers' brand evaluations are defined as customers' general affective assessment of a brand.

Source: Wu, L., King, C. A., Lu, L. & Guchait, P. (2020). Hospitality aesthetic labor management: Consumers' and prospective employees' perspectives of hospitality brands. *International Journal of Hospitality Management*, *87*, 102373.

Consumers' enduring cultural involvement

Definition: Consumers' enduring cultural involvement is defined as the consumers' enduring interest and arousal toward a particular culture being represented by a brand.

> **Source:** Jian, Y., Zhou, Z. & Zhou, N. (2019). Brand cultural symbolism, brand authenticity, and consumer well-being: the moderating role of cultural involvement. *Journal of Product & Brand Management, 28*(4), 529-539.

Consumer expertise

Definition: Consumer expertise was defined as the extent to which a communicator is perceived to be a source of valid assertions.

> **Source:** Zhang, B., Ritchie, B., Mair, J. & Driml, S. (2019). Is the Airline Trustworthy? The Impact of Source Credibility on Voluntary Carbon Offsetting. *Journal of Travel Research, 58*(5), 715-731.

Consumption collectives

Definition: Consumption collectives can be defined as collectives of consumers who share
the same consumption objects and/or practices, engage in loops of learning and create and
co-produce content surrounding the brand.

> **Source:** Närvänen, E. & Goulding, C. (2016). Sociocultural brand revitalization: The role of consumer collectives in bringing brands back to life. *European Journal of Marketing, 50*(7/8), 1521-1546.

Content quality

Definition: Content quality can be defined as consumer's perception of the accuracy, completeness, relevance and timeliness of brand-related information on the brands' social media page.

> **Source:** Dabbous, A. & Barakat, K. A. (2020). Bridging the online offline gap: Assessing the impact of brands' social network content quality on brand awareness and purchase intention. *Journal of Retailing and Consumer Services, 53*, 101966.

Continuance intention to follow

Definition: Continuance intention to follow is related to the intention of followers to maintain a relationship with the brand or micro-blog, which indicates a form of post-adoption behavior.

> **Source:** Zhao, H., Su, C. & Hua, Z. (2016). Investigating continuance intention to follow a brand micro-blog:Perceived value and social identification. *Information Development, 32*(5), 1428-1441.

Convenience

Definition: Convenience is defined as a reduction in the amount of consumer time and/or energy required to acquire, use, and dispose or a product or service relative to the time and energy required by other offerings in the product/service class.

> **Source:** Bazi, S., Filieri, R. & Gorton, M. (2020). Customers' motivation to engage with luxury brands on social media. *Journal of Business Research, 112*, 223-235.

Conversational human voice

Definition: Conversational human voice is defined as an engaging and natural style of organizational communication as perceived by an organization's publics based on interactions between individuals in the organization.

> **Source:** Gretry, A., Horváth, C., Belei, N. & van Riel, A. C. R. (2017). "Don't pretend to be my friend!" When an informal brand communication style backfires on social media. *Journal of Business Research, 74*, 77-89.

Copycat brand

Definition: Copycat brands refer to those that imitate features of leading brands so as to free ride on their high brand equity.

> **Source:** Qin, Y., Wen, N., and Dou, W. (2016) Effects of perceptual and conceptual similarities on consumers' evaluations of copycat brand names. *J. Consumer Behaviour., 15*: 117– 125

Corporate associations

Definition: Corporate associations refer to all information held by an individual on a firm which may include perceptions, inferences and beliefs about a firm; an individual's general knowledge of the firm.

> **Source:** Jeon Jung, O. & Baeck, S. (2016). What drives consumer's responses to brand crisis? The moderating roles of brand associations and brand-customer relationship strength. *Journal of Product & Brand Management, 25*(6), 550-567.

Corporate brand

Definition: Corporate brand is described as firms that will deliver and stand behind the offering that the customer will buy and use. Corporate brands typically are founded on a relatively "small set of fundamental core values".

> **Source:** Voss, K. E. & Mohan, M. (2016). Corporate brand effects in brand alliances. *Journal of Business Research, 69*(10), 4177-4184.

Corporate social responsibility

Definition: Corporate social responsibility refers to a firm's obligation to society or the extent of a firm's activities and status related to its perceived societal or stakeholder obligations.

Source: Vuong, B. N. & Khanh Giao, H. N. (2020). The Impact of Perceived Brand Globalness on Consumers' Purchase Intention and the Moderating Role of Consumer Ethnocentrism: An Evidence from Vietnam. *Journal of International Consumer Marketing*, 32(1), 47-68.

Correspondence bias

Definition: Correspondence bias is defined as the tendency to draw inferences about a person's unique and enduring dispositions from behaviors that can be entirely explained by the situations in which they occur.

Source: Kang, J. (2020). The Effect of Ad Skepticism and Celebrity Preference on Brand Attitude Change in Celebrity-Endorsed Advertising. *Japanese Psychological Research*, 62(1), 26-38.

Country of origin image

Definition (1): Country of origin image is defined as the sum of associations about products (and brands) from a given country.

Source: Allman, H. F., Fenik, A. P., Hewett, K. & Morgan, F. N. (2016). Brand Image Evaluations: The Interactive Roles of Country of Manufacture, Brand Concept, and Vertical Line Extension Type. *Journal of International Marketing*, 24(2), 40-61.

Definition (2): Country of origin is defined as the entire evaluation by a consumer of products from a specific country, based on past evaluation of that country's products.

Source: Abalkhail, T. S. (2018). The Attitudes of Saudi Youth Toward U.S. Apparel Brand Names. *Journal of International Consumer Marketing*, 30(1), 58-68.

Credibility

Definition: Credibility indicates a customer's perception that the words and promises of a service firm can be trusted, whereas benevolence indicates a customer's belief that a service firm's motives and intents are beneficial to its customers.

Source: Agyei, J., Sun, S., Abrokwah, E., Penney, E. K. & Ofori-Boafo, R. (2020). Influence of Trust on Customer Engagement: Empirical Evidence From the Insurance Industry in Ghana. *SAGE Open*, 10(1), 2158244019899104.

Credibility of a brand

Definition: Credibility of a brand is defined as the brand's transparency and honesty toward the consumer, as well as its willingness and ability to fulfill its claims.

Source: Charlton, A. B. & Cornwell, T. B. (2019). Authenticity in horizontal marketing partnerships: A better measure of brand compatibility. *Journal of Business Research*, 100, 279-298.

Customer brand satisfaction

Definition: Customer satisfaction is defined as consumer's pleasurable fulfilment response and it expresses the favorable affective response of customers who find all past service encounters with their service providers rewarding.

> **Source:** Giovanis, A. N. & Athanasopoulou, P. (2018). Consumer-brand relationships and brand loyalty in technology-mediated services. *Journal of Retailing and Consumer Services, 40,* 287-294.

Customer brand engagement

Definition (1): Customer brand engagement is described as the customers' cognitive, affective and behavioural investment in specific brand interactions which emerges as a dynamic process that envolves in three progressive relational phases: friendship, intimacy and symbiosis.

> **Source:** Kumar, J. & Nayak Jogendra, K. (2019). Brand engagement without brand ownership: a case of non-brand owner community members. *Journal of Product & Brand Management, 28*(2), 216-230.

Definition (2): Customer brand engagement is a psychological state that occurs by virtue of interactive, co-creative customer experiences with a focal agent/object (e.g., a brand) in focal service relationships.

> **Source:** Cheng, Y.-Y., Tung, W.-F., Yang, M.-H. & Chiang, C.-T. (2019). Linking relationship equity to brand resonance in a social networking brand community. *Electronic Commerce Research and Applications, 35,* 100849.

Definition (3): Customer brand engagement is defined as the level of a customer's motivational, brand-related and context-dependent state of mind characterised by specific levels of cognitive, emotional and behavioural activity in brand interactions.

> **Source:** Garg, P., Gupta, B., Dzever, S., Sivarajah, U. & Kumar, V. (2020). Examining the Relationship between Social Media Analytics Practices and Business Performance in the Indian Retail and IT Industries: The Mediation Role of Customer Engagement. *International Journal of Information Management, 52,* 102069.

Customer brand identification

Definition: Customer brand identification is a multidimensional construct that consists of a cognitive component (i.e., cognitive awareness of membership), and emotional component (i.e., affective investment in the awareness and evaluations).

> **Source:** So, K. K. F., Wu, L., Xiong, L. & King, C. (2018). Brand Management in the Era of Social Media: Social Visibility of Consumption and Customer Brand Identification. *Journal of Travel Research, 57*(6), 727-742.

Customer citizenship behavior

Definition: Customer citizenship behaviour is defined as helpful, constructive gestures exhibited by customers that are valued or appreciated by the firm, but not related directly to enforceable or explicit requirements of the individual's role.

> **Source:** Mandl, L. & Hogreve, J. (2020). Buffering effects of brand community identification in service failures: The role of customer citizenship behaviors. *Journal of Business Research, 107*, 130-137.

Customer engagement

Definition (1): Customer engagement is considered in the literature as an ongoing relationship between a brand and a customer.

> **Source:** Gómez Suárez, M. (2018). Examining Customer-Brand Relationships: A Critical Approach to Empirical Models on Brand Attachment, Love, and Engagement. *Administrative Sciences, 9.*

Definition (2): Customer Engagement is a customer's personal connection to a brand as manifested in cognitive, affective, and behavioral responses outside of the purchase.

> **Source:** Swoboda, B., Puchert, C. & Morschett, D. (2016). Explaining the differing effects of corporate reputation across nations: a multilevel analysis. *Journal of the Academy of Marketing Science, 44*(4), 454-473.

Definition (3): Customer engagement is defined as a set of customer behaviors vis-à-vis the firm – both transactional (loyalty, repurchase intention) and non-transactional (commitment, word-of-mouth, referrals, blogging, etc.) in nature – which guarantee future sales.

> **Source:** Garg, P., Gupta, B., Dzever, S., Sivarajah, U. & Kumar, V. (2020). Examining the Relationship between Social Media Analytics Practices and Business Performance in the Indian Retail and IT Industries: The Mediation Role of Customer Engagement. *International Journal of Information Management, 52*, 102069.

Customer equity

Definition: Customer equity is a multidimensional construct that encompasses value equity, brand equity and relationship quality.

> **Source:** Gao, L., Melero-Polo, I. & Sese, F. J. (2020). Customer Equity Drivers, Customer Experience Quality, and Customer Profitability in Banking Services: The Moderating Role of Social Influence. *Journal of Service Research, 23*(2), 174-193.

Customer ethnocentrism

Definition: Customer Ethnocentrism is viewed as the beliefs held by consumers about the appropriateness, indeed morality, of purchasing foreign-made products.

> **Source:** Balabanis, G. & Siamagka, N.-T. (2017). Inconsistencies in the behavioural effects of consumer ethnocentrism: The role of brand, product category and country of origin. *International Marketing Review, 34*(2), 166-182.

Customer experience

Definition (1): Customer experience is defined as "the customer's interpretation of his or her total interaction with the brand and perceived value of this encounter.

> **Source:** Zhang, J., Jiang, Y., Shabbir, R. & Zhu, M. (2016). How brand orientation impacts B2B service brand equity? An empirical study among Chinese firms. *Journal of Business & Industrial Marketing, 31*(1), 83-98.

Definition (2): Customer experience is the aggregate and cumulative customer perception created during learning about, acquiring, using, maintaining and disposing of a product or service.

> **Source:** Trivedi, J. (2019). Examining the Customer Experience of Using Banking Chatbots and Its Impact on Brand Love: The Moderating Role of Perceived Risk. *Journal of Internet Commerce, 18*(1), 91-111.

Definition (3): Customer experience can be defined as the subjective response to the holistic direct and indirect encounter with the firm which encompasses every aspect of a company's offering, including the quality of customer care, advertising, packaging and product.

> **Source:** Gao, L., Melero-Polo, I. & Sese, F. J. (2020). Customer Equity Drivers, Customer Experience Quality, and Customer Profitability in Banking Services: The Moderating Role of Social Influence. *Journal of Service Research, 23*(2), 174-193.

Customer experience quality

Definition: Customer experience quality can be understood as the perceived judgment about the excellence or superiority of the customer experience.

> **Source:** Gao, L., Melero-Polo, I. & Sese, F. J. (2020). Customer Equity Drivers, Customer Experience Quality, and Customer Profitability in Banking Services: The Moderating Role of Social Influence. *Journal of Service Research, 23*(2), 174-193.

Customer lifetime value

Definition: Customer lifetime value incorporates the total amount of revenue generated from the loyalty program members and the total cost invested in the loyalty program by the company.

Source: Yoo, M., Bai, B. & Singh, A. (2020). The evolution of behavioral loyalty and customer lifetime value over time: investigation from a Casino Loyalty Program. *Journal of Marketing Analytics*, 8(2), 45-56.

Customer participation

Definition: Customer participation is a construct that contains two dimensions about the brand: the search for information, and the sharing of information.

Source: González-Mansilla, Ó., Berenguer-Contrí, G. & Serra-Cantallops, A. (2019). The impact of value co-creation on hotel brand equity and customer satisfaction. *Tourism Management*, 75, 51-65.

Customer profitability

Definition: Customer profitability is conceptualized as the difference between customer revenues and costs, which are central components in the calculation of customer lifetime value.

Source: Gao, L., Melero-Polo, I. & Sese, F. J. (2020). Customer Equity Drivers, Customer Experience Quality, and Customer Profitability in Banking Services: The Moderating Role of Social Influence. *Journal of Service Research*, 23(2), 174-193.

Customer referral programs

Definition: Customer referral programs are defined as a form of stimulated Word of mouth that provides incentives to existing customers to bring in new customers.

Source: Stumpf, C. & Baum, M. (2016). Customer Referral Reward–Brand–Fit: A Schema Congruity Perspective. *Psychology & Marketing*, 33(7), 542-558.

Customer-based brand equity,

Definition: Customer-based brand equity, refers to the additional value provided by a brand name to a product or service, manifests through cognitive and behavioral preferences such as the brand's perceived level of distinctiveness within the service category.

Source: Wu, L., King, C. A., Lu, L. & Guchait, P. (2020). Hospitality aesthetic labor management: Consumers' and prospective employees' perspectives of hospitality brands. *International Journal of Hospitality Management*, 87, 102373.

Customer-brand identification

Definition: Customer-brand identification is defined as a customer's psychological state of perceiving, feeling, and valuing his or her belongingness with a brand.

Source: Vahdati, Y. & Voss Kevin, E. (2019). Brand identification, cause-brand alliances and perceived cause controversy. *Journal of Product & Brand Management*, *28*(7), 880-892.

Customization

Definition: Customization has been defined as activities where users themselves modify some aspect of an interface (or product) to a certain degree so as to increase its personal relevance.

Source: Bazi, S., Filieri, R. & Gorton, M. (2020). Customers' motivation to engage with luxury brands on social media. *Journal of Business Research*, *112*, 223-235.

Cuteness

Definition: Cuteness is defined as being attractive in an adorable or endearing way. Cuteness is a broad concept in which attributes such as shapes, colours and design may also evoke adorable and affective feelings.

Source: Lee Crystal, T. & Hsieh Sara, H. (2019). Engaging consumers in mobile instant messaging: the role of cute branded emoticons. *Journal of Product & Brand Management*, *28*(7), 849-863.

Design quality

Definition: Design quality entails the perception of the balance, emotional appeal, aesthetics, and uniformity of a website's overall visual look.

Source: Kim, Y. & Peterson, R. A. (2017). A Meta-analysis of Online Trust Relationships in E-commerce. *Journal of Interactive Marketing*, *38*, 44-54.

Desire for reconciliation

Definition: Desire for reconciliation is defined as a customer's willingness to accept a firm's failure and to extend acts of goodwill in the hope of maintaining a relationship with the firm.

Source: Sheraz, A. & Sharizal, b. H. (2018). The moderating effect of brand recovery on brand hate and desire for reconciliation: A PLS-MGA approach. *International Journal of Business and Society*, Vol. 19 No. 3

Desire for unique products

Definition: Desire for unique products refers to the extent to which different consumers hold as a personal goal of acquiring and processing products, services, and experiences that few others possess.

Source: Shim, C., Kang, S., Kim, I. & Hyun, S. S. (2017). Luxury-cruise travellers' brand community perception and its consequences. *Current Issues in Tourism*, *20*(14), 1489-1509.

Destination branding

Definition: Destination branding is the marketing activities which support the creation of name, logo, word, or mark that differentiates a destination so as to convey the expectation of a memorable travel experience and to strengthen the emotional connection between the detination brand and tourists.

> Source: Wong, P. P. W. (2018). Role of components of destination competitiveness in the relationship between customer-based brand equity and destination loyalty. *Current Issues in Tourism*, 21(5), 504-528.

Dynamic brand logo

Definition: Dynamic brand logo is a brand logo with motion along with an applied drag force.

> Source: Baxter, S. M. & Ilicic, J. (2018). May the force drag your dynamic logo: The brand work-energy effect. *International Journal of Research in Marketing*, 35(3), 509-523.

Ease of use

Definition: Ease of use is a construct of the technology acceptance model (TAM) who defines it as the degree to which a person believes that using a particular system would be free of effort.

> Source: Bazi, S., Filieri, R. & Gorton, M. (2020). Customers' motivation to engage with luxury brands on social media. *Journal of Business Research*, 112, 223-235.

Efficiency

Definition: Efficiency refers to the relationship between inputs and outputs.

> Source: Rahman, M., Rodríguez-Serrano, M. Á. & Lambkin, M. (2018). Brand management efficiency and firm value: An integrated resource based and signalling theory perspective. *Industrial Marketing Management*, 72, 112-126.

Electronic Word of mouth

Definition: Electronic word of mouth is commonly defined as any form of positive or negative statement about a product, service or company, produced by consumers and made publicly available through web-based services such as e.g., social media, websites, reviews.

> Source: Ilhan, B. E., Kübler, R. V. & Pauwels, K. H. (2018). Battle of the Brand Fans: Impact of Brand Attack and Defense on Social Media. *Journal of Interactive Marketing*, 43, 33-51.

Elitism

Definition: Elitism is defined as perceived expensiveness and limited dissemination of luxury brands.

> Source: Roux, E., Tafani, E. & Vigneron, F. (2017). Values associated with luxury brand consumption and the role of gender. *Journal of Business Research, 71*, 102-113.

Emotional brand attachment

Definition: Emotional brand attachment is an emotion-laden target-specific bond between a person and a specific object or brand.

> Source: Gómez Suárez, M. (2018). Examining Customer-Brand Relationships: A Critical Approach to Empirical Models on Brand Attachment, Love, and Engagement. *Administrative Sciences, 9*.

Emotional brand attraction

Definition: Emotional brand attraction is the holistic perception of a power of seduction to a brand which grants it an important aesthetic value and which makes that any contact with it gets strong sensations and pleasure.

> Source: Shim, C., Kang, S., Kim, I. & Hyun, S. S. (2017). Luxury-cruise travellers' brand community perception and its consequences. *Current Issues in Tourism, 20*(14), 1489-1509.

Emotional brand experience

Definition: Emotional brand experience is the subjective, internal and behavioral responses evoked by brandrelated stimuli that are part of a brand's design, identity, packaging, communication, and environment.

> Source: Bapat, D. (2017). Impact of brand familiarity on brands experience dimensions for financial services brands. *International Journal of Bank Marketing, 35*(4), 637-648.

Emotional brand relationship

Definition: Emotional brand relationships is conceptualised using self-concept connection, emotional attachment and brand love.

> Source: Pourazad, N., Stocchi, L. & Pare, V. (2019). Brand attribute associations, emotional consumer-brand relationship and evaluation of brand extensions. *Australasian Marketing Journal (AMJ), 27*(4), 249-260.

Emotional branding

Definition: Emotional branding is the strategies to create an emotional brand (e.g. sensory branding, storytelling, cause branding, and customer empowerment)

> Source: Kim, Y.-K. & Sullivan, P. (2019). Emotional branding speaks to consumers' heart: the case of fashion brands. *Fashion and Textiles, 6*(1), 2.

Emotional exhaustion

Definition: Emotional exhaustion is referred to as the extent to which employees feel emotionally overwhelmed and drained by their work.

> **Source:** Wong, I. A., Xu, S., Chan, S. H. G. & He, M. (2019). A cross-level investigation of the role of human resources practices: Does brand equity matter? *Tourism Management, 75,* 418-426.

Employee brand equity

Definition: Employee-based brand equity is defined as the differential effect that brand knowledge has on an employee's response to their work environment.

> **Source:** Altaf, M., Mokhtar, S. & Ghani, N. (2019). Employee Brand Equity : Mediating Role of Brand Role Clarity and Employee Brand Commitment. P*ertanika Journal of Social Science and Humanities* 27, 165-175

Employees' static appearance

Definition: Employees' static appearance consists of dress style and bodily characteristics. which encompasses uniform design and employees' personal grooming.

> **Source:** Wu, L., King, C. A., Lu, L. & Guchait, P. (2020). Hospitality aesthetic labor management: Consumers' and prospective employees' perspectives of hospitality brands. *International Journal of Hospitality Management, 87,* 102373.

Employees' value congruence

Definition: Employees' value congruence is defined as the extent to which there is congruency between employees' personal values and those communicated by the company.

> **Source:** Hu, Y., Ma, Z. & Kim, H. J. (2018). Examining Effects of Internal Branding on Hospitality Student Interns' Brand-Supportive Behaviors: The Role of Value Congruence. *Journal of Hospitality & Tourism Education, 30*(3), 144-153.

Employer brand equity

Definition: Employer brand equity can be described as applicants' beliefs about a company as an employer based on their knowledge about and experiences with a company.

> **Source:** Stockman, S.; Hoye, G.; Veiga, S. (2020) Negative word-of-mouth and applicant attraction: The role of employer brand equity. Journal of Vocational Behaviour, 103368

Enegetic brand

Definition: Energetic brand is defined as a brand that possesses strong enthusiasm, energy and vigour.

Source: Warren, C., Batra, R., Loureiro, S. M. C. & Bagozzi, R. P. (2019). Brand Coolness. *Journal of Marketing*, 83(5), 36-56.

Endorser attractiveness

Definition: The attractiveness of a celebrity endorser (endorser attractiveness) is defined as celebrity physical appearance and beauty.

Source: Kang, J. & Choi, W. J. (2016). Endorsed Sustainable Products: The Role of Celebrity Ethicality and Brand Ethicality. *Clothing and Textiles Research Journal*, 34(4), 303-319.

Endorser brand congruity

Definition: Endorser-brand congruity is defined as the degree of match between accessible endorser associations and attributes associated with the brand'.

Source: Kang, J. & Choi, W. J. (2016). Endorsed Sustainable Products: The Role of Celebrity Ethicality and Brand Ethicality. *Clothing and Textiles Research Journal*, 34(4), 303-319.

Endorser ethicality

Definition: Endorser ethicality is defined as the extent to which a celebrity endorser is perceived as responsible, fair, and transparent.

Source: Kang, J. & Choi, W. J. (2016). Endorsed Sustainable Products: The Role of Celebrity Ethicality and Brand Ethicality. *Clothing and Textiles Research Journal*, 34(4), 303-319.

Endorser trustworthiness

Definition: trustworthiness of a celebrity endorser (endorser trustworthiness) is the
extent to which the celebrity is perceived as honest and believable.

Source: Kang, J. & Choi, W. J. (2016). Endorsed Sustainable Products: The Role of Celebrity Ethicality and Brand Ethicality. *Clothing and Textiles Research Journal*, 34(4), 303-319.

Enduring involvement

Definition: Enduring involvement is defined as an individual variable representing
the arousal potential of a product or activity that causes personal relevance.

Source: Vashist, D. (2018). Effect of product involvement and brand prominence on advergamers' brand recall and brand attitude in an emerging market context. *Asia Pacific Journal of Marketing and Logistics*, 30(1), 43-61.

Energetic brand

Definition: Energetic brand is defined as a brand that possesses strong enthusiasm, energy and vigor.

>**Source:** Warren, C., Batra, R., Loureiro, S. M. C. & Bagozzi, R. P. (2019). Brand Coolness. *Journal of Marketing*, 83(5), 36-56.

Entertainment

Definition: Entertainment is defined as escaping or being diverted from problems or routine; emotional release or relief; relaxation; cultural or aesthetic enjoyment; passing time; and sexual arousal.

>**Source:** Bazi, S., Filieri, R. & Gorton, M. (2020). Customers' motivation to engage with luxury brands on social media. *Journal of Business Research*, 112, 223-235.

Event image

Definition: Event image is "the cumulative interpretation of meanings or associations attributed to events by consumers. Also, event image is a cognitive construction associating rational and affective representations of an event by a person or a group.

>**Source:** Yu & Kim. (2020). The Relationship between Self-City Brand Connection, City Brand Experience, and City Brand Ambassadors. *Sustainability*, 12, 982.

Electronic word of mouth

Definition: Electronic word of mouth is the consumer-generated, consumption-related communication that employs digital tools and is directed primarily to other consumers.

>**Source:** Sagynbekova, S., Ince, E., Ogunmokun, O. A., Olaoke, R. O. & Ukeje, U. E. (2021). Social media communication and higher education brand equity: The mediating role of eWOM. *Journal of Public Affairs*, e2112.

Existential authenticity

Definition: Existential authenticity can be defined as a state of existence in which one is true to oneself.

>**Source:** Mody, M. & Hanks, L. (2020). Consumption Authenticity in the Accommodations Industry: The Keys to Brand Love and Brand Loyalty for Hotels and Airbnb. *Journal of Travel Research*, 59(1), 173-189.

Extraordinary brand

Definition: Extraordinary brand is defined as a positive quality that sets a brand apart from its competitors or offer a superior functional value.

>**Source:** Warren, C., Batra, R., Loureiro, S. M. C. & Bagozzi, R. P. (2019). Brand Coolness.

Journal of Marketing, 83(5), 36-56.

Familiarity

Definition: Familiarity is defined as an individual's familiarity with the source through any media exposure.

> **Source:** Cuomo, M., Foroudi, P., Tortora, D., Hussain, S. & Melewar, T. C. (2019). Celebrity Endorsement and the Attitude Towards Luxury Brands for Sustainable Consumption. *Sustainability*, *11*, 6791.

Family business brand

Definition: Family business brand is the formal and informal communication (image) of the family element of firm essence (identity), which includes the family's involvement in a firm, and which lead to associations and expectations in the mind of stakeholders.

> **Source:** Lude, M. & Prügl, R. (2018). Why the family business brand matters: Brand authenticity and the family firm trust inference. *Journal of Business Research*, *89*, 121-134.

Felt responsibility

Definition: Felt responsibility is a psychological state underlying creative behaviour and denotes employee commitment to the continuous generation of performance-oriented change beyond the base execution of responsibilities according to established standards.

> **Source:** Campbell, J. W. (2018). Felt responsibility for change in public organizations: general and sector-specific paths. *Public Management Review*, *20*(2), 232-253.

Firm product innovation

Definition: Firm product innovation refers to the firm product type, quality and performance aspects of targeted improvement or creation and at the right time to put it into the market

> **Source:** Zameer, H., Wang, Y. & Yasmeen, H. (2019). Transformation of firm innovation activities into brand effect. *Marketing Intelligence & Planning*, *37*(2), 226-240.

Franchisee-based brand equity

Definition: Franchisee-based brand equity is a set of assets and liabilities linked to a brand, its name and symbol that adds to or subtracts from the value provided by a product or service to a franchisee.

> **Source:** Nyadzayo, M. W., Matanda, M. J. & Ewing, M. T. (2016). Franchisee-based brand equity: The role of brand relationship quality and brand citizenship behavior. *Industrial Marketing Management*, *52*, 163-174.

Franchising

Definition: Franchising is a business format wherein a firm (i.e., the franchisee) enters a long-term contractual agreement with another firm (i.e., the franchisor) in order to market products or services under brand names and business practices defined by franchisor.

> **Source:** Badrinarayanan, V., Suh, T. & Kim, K.-M. (2016). Brand resonance in franchising relationships: A franchisee-based perspective. *Journal of Business Research*, 69(10), 3943-3950.

Functional brand qualities

Definition: Functional qualities refers to the qualities of products that have a more utilitarian, tangible or rational nature, that is, that are more closely aligned with a products' physical characteristics, and that, as such, are relatively objective features.

> **Source:** Coelho, F. J. F., Bairrada, C. M. & de Matos Coelho, A. F. (2020). Functional brand qualities and perceived value: The mediating role of brand experience and brand personality. *Psychology & Marketing*, 37(1), 41-55.

Functional utility

Definition: Functional utility refers to the practical benefits of brands that are tangible.

> **Source:** Davari, A., Iyer, P. & Guzmán, F. (2017). Determinants of brand resurrection movements: Why consumers want dead brands back? *European Journal of Marketing*, 51(11/12), 1896-1917.

Global brand

Definition (1): Global brand is perceived as global and marketed not only locally but also in some foreign markets. A global brand is a brand that is standardized across countries with worldwide recognition and availability.

> **Source:** Trivedi, J. (2019). Examining the Customer Experience of Using Banking Chatbots and Its Impact on Brand Love: The Moderating Role of Perceived Risk. *Journal of Internet Commerce*, 18(1), 91-111.

Definition (2): Global brands are brands that have widespread regional/global awareness, availability, acceptance, and demand and are often found under the same name with consistent positioning, personality, look, and feel in major markets enabled by centrally coordinated marketing actions.

> **Source:** Molinillo, S., Japutra, A., Nguyen, B. & Chen Cheng-Hao, S. (2017). Responsible brands vs active brands? An examination of brand personality on brand awareness, brand trust, and brand loyalty. *Marketing Intelligence & Planning*, 35(2), 166-179.

Green brand

Definition: Green brand is alternatively expressed as eco-friendly brands, "environmentally friendly brand, or sustainable brands, and is defined as products ands services that lessen health and environmental impacts compared to similar products and services.

> **Source:** Kang Ju-Young, M. & Kim, J. (2017). Online customer relationship marketing tactics through social media and perceived customer retention orientation of the green retailer. *Journal of Fashion Marketing and Management: An International Journal, 21*(3), 298-316.

Green brand positioning

Definition: Green brand positioning refers to marketing activities, which use environmental issues to distinguish a brand's products from other brands.

> **Source:** Jeng, M.-Y. & Yeh, T.-M. (2016). The effect of consumer values on the brand position of green restaurants by means-end chain and laddering interviews. *Service Business, 10*(1), 223-238.

Halo effect

Definition: Halo effect is characteristically conceptualized as a global attitude toward an object that imbues beliefs about the object.

> **Source:** Lee, R., Lockshin, L., Cohen, J. & Corsi, A. (2019). A latent growth model of destination image's halo effect. *Annals of Tourism Research, 79*, 102767.

Harmounious passion

Definition: Harmonious passion is a strong inclination toward an activity that people like, that they find important, and in which they invest time and energy.

> **Source:** Moulard, J. G., Raggio, R. D. & Folse, J. A. G. (2016). Brand Authenticity: Testing the Antecedents and Outcomes of Brand Management's Passion for its Products. *Psychology & Marketing, 33*(6), 421-436.

Hate

Definition: Hate is considered as a result from two primary emotions, that is, disgust and anger.

> **Source:** Zarantonello, L., Romani, S., Grappi, S. & Bagozzi Richard, P. (2016). Brand hate. *Journal of Product & Brand Management, 25*(1), 11-25.

Hedonic attributes

Definition: Hedonic attributes refer to benefits such as the feelings of fun, pleasure and enjoyment that a consumer may gain through owning or consuming a brand.

Source: Pourazad, N., Stocchi, L. & Pare, V. (2019). Brand attribute associations, emotional consumer-brand relationship and evaluation of brand extensions. *Australasian Marketing Journal (AMJ)*, 27(4), 249-260.

Hedonic motivation

Definition: Hedonic motivation refers to the entertainment factor associated with certain activities as the result of the fun and play.

Source: Dabbous, A. & Barakat, K. A. (2020). Bridging the online offline gap: Assessing the impact of brands' social network content quality on brand awareness and purchase intention. *Journal of Retailing and Consumer Services*, 53, 101966.

Helping behaviour

Definition: Helping behavior is related to customers' actions toward a brand and it is defined as positive attitudes, helpfulness, exhibiting empathy and friendliness toward a brand.

Source: Kim, S.-H., Kim, M. & Lee, S. (2019). The consumer value-based brand citizenship behavior model: Evidence from local and global coffee businesses. *Journal of Hospitality Marketing & Management*, 28(4), 472-490.

Homophily

Definition: Homophily was used to describe a tendency for friendships to form between those who are alike in some designated respect

Source: Watkins, L., Aitken, R., Thyne, M., Robertson, K. & Borzekowski, D. (2017). Environmental influences on pre-schooler's understanding of brand symbolism. *Marketing Intelligence & Planning*, 35(7), 907-922.

Humor appreciation

Definition: Humor appreciation is defned as the psychological state characterized by amusement, the tendency to laugh and the perception that something is funny

Source: Duong, G. H., Wu, W.-Y. & Le, L. H. (2020). The effects of brand page characteristics on customer brand engagement: moderating roles of community involvement and comedy production contents. *Journal of Brand Management*, 27(5), 531-545.

Iconic brand

Definition: Iconic Brand is a brand widely recognized as a cultural symbol.

Source: Warren, C., Batra, R., Loureiro, S. M. C. & Bagozzi, R. P. (2019). Brand Coolness. *Journal of Marketing*, 83(5), 36-56.

Ideal self

Definition: Ideal self refers to the individual's aspirational self, which manifests a vision of ideals and goals related to his or her future self (i.e., who I would like to be).

> **Source:** Kim, Y.-K. & Sullivan, P. (2019). Emotional branding speaks to consumers heart: the case of fashion brands. *Fashion and Textiles*, 6(1), 2.

Image

Definition: Image is a sum of beliefs, attitudes, and impressions that a person perceives toward an object or a brand. Images are shaped by brand attitude.

> **Source:** Shin, H., Lee, H. & Perdue, R. R. (2018). The congruity effects of commercial brand sponsorship in a regional event. *Tourism Management*, 67, 168-179.

Information processing

Definition: Information processing is the extent to which a reader engages a text or the amount of interpretation occasioned by a text or the number of inferences drawn.

> **Source:** Ahn, J. & Back, K.-J. (2020). The structural effects of affective and cognitive elaboration in formation of customer–brand relationship. *The Service Industries Journal*, 40(3-4), 226-242.

Information quality

Definition: Information quality or argument quality refers to the persuasive strength of arguments embedded in an informational message.

> **Source:** Sijoria, C., Mukherjee, S. & Datta, B. (2018). Impact of the antecedents of eWOM on CBBE. *Marketing Intelligence & Planning*, 36(5), 528-542.

Information quantity

Definition: Information quantity is the extent or volume of information about a brand.

> **Source:** Sijoria, C., Mukherjee, S. & Datta, B. (2018). Impact of the antecedents of eWOM on CBBE. *Marketing Intelligence & Planning*, 36(5), 528-542.

Information usefulness

Definition: Information usefulness is conceptualized as the degree to which information provides useful content that adds economic or functional utility to consumers.

> **Source:** Zhao, H., Su, C. & Hua, Z. (2016). Investigating continuance intention to follow a brand micro-blog:Perceived value and social identification. *Information Development*, 32(5), 1428-1441.

Informativeness

Definition: Informativeness is the relevance and usefulness of given information for potential applicants who want to evaluate the organization.

> Source: Carpentier, M., Van Hoye, G. & Weijters, B. (2019). Attracting applicants through the organization's social media page: Signaling employer brand personality. *Journal of Vocational Behavior*, 115, 103326.

Innovation orientation

Definition: Innovation orientation refers to the distinct organisational values and behaviours that reflect a willingness to innovate and adopt new forms of innovation.

> Source: Bridson, K. C. & Evans, J. (2018). Brand compass: charting a course to improve firm performance. *Journal of Strategic Marketing*, 26(2), 174-187.

Integrity

Definition: Integrity is noticed when the brand displays a deep commitment to the best interests of its customers, holding customers' interests even above its own and at the heart of the organization.

> Source: Portal, S., Abratt, R. & Bendixen, M. (2018). Building a human brand: Brand anthropomorphism unravelled. *Business Horizons*, 61(3), 367-374.

Intellectual experience

Definition: Intellectual experience is achieved when consumers' curiosity and thoughts are stimulated by a brand's intellectual appeals (e.g., technology used in service delivery and new product promotions).

> Source: Kang, J., Kwun, D. J. & Hahm, J. J. (2020). Turning Your Customers into Brand Evangelists: Evidence from Cruise Travelers. *Journal of Quality Assurance in Hospitality & Tourism*, 21(6), 617-643.

Interdependent self-construal

Definition: Interdependent self-construal is defined as a social orientation that emphasizes an individual's embeddedness and connectedness with others

> Source: Sugitani, Y. (2018). The Effect of Self- and Public-Based Evaluations on Brand Purchasing: The Interplay of Independent and Interdependent Self-Construal. *Journal of International Consumer Marketing*, 30(4), 235-243.

Internal branding

Definition (1): Internal branding is defined as the concerted, inter-departmental and multi-directional internal communications effort carried out in order to create and maintain an internal brand. Internal branding attempts to achieve consistency with the external brand.

> **Source:** Hu, Y., Ma, Z. & Kim, H. J. (2018). Examining Effects of Internal Branding on Hospitality Student Interns' Brand-Supportive Behaviors: The Role of Value Congruence. *Journal of Hospitality & Tourism Education, 30*(3), 144-153.

Definition (2): Internal branding has been considered as a mechanism for enhancing employees' identification with organizations to accomplish the organization's strategic interest, with an aim of achieving congruency between internal and external brand messages.

> **Source:** Yu, Q., Asaad, Y., Yen, D. A. & Gupta, S. (2018). IMO and internal branding outcomes: an employee perspective in UK HE. *Studies in Higher Education, 43*(1), 37-56.

Definition (3): Internal branding refers to brand-building efforts that focus on promoting a brand inside an organization to motive the employees to transform the brand promise into reality.

> **Source:** Xie, L., Li, Y., Chen, S.-H. & Huan, T.-C. (2016). Triad theory of hotel managerial leadership, employee brand-building behavior, and guest images of luxury-hotel brands. *International Journal of Contemporary Hospitality Management, 28*(9), 1826-1847.

Definition (4): Internal branding is defined as the set of strategic processes that align and empower employees to deliver the appropriate customer experience in a consistent fashion.

> **Source:** Zhang, J., Jiang, Y., Shabbir, R. & Zhu, M. (2016). How brand orientation impacts B2B service brand equity? An empirical study among Chinese firms. *Journal of Business & Industrial Marketing, 31*(1), 83-98.

Interpersonal influence

Definition: Interpersonal influence is based on the desire to make informed decisions and is defined as the tendency to accept information from others as credible evidence of reality.

> **Source:** Yang, K., Kim, J. & Kim, Y.-K. (2017). The effect of brand consciousness on interpersonal influences, brand values, and purchase intention: Cases for American and Korean college students. *Journal of Global Fashion Marketing, 8*(2), 83-97.

Intimacy

Definition: Intimacy defines as a deep understanding of relationship partners created through information disclosure, reducing uncertainty.

> **Source:** Jeon Jung, O. & Baeck, S. (2016). What drives consumer's responses to brand crisis? The moderating roles of brand associations and brand-customer relationship strength. *Journal of Product & Brand Management, 25*(6), 550-567.

Intrapersonal authenticity

Definition: Intrapersonal authenticity is related to the individual self, and includes physical aspects (for example relaxation and invigoration), and psychological aspects, such as self-discovery and self-realization.

> **Source:** Mody, M. & Hanks, L. (2020). Consumption Authenticity in the Accommodations Industry: The Keys to Brand Love and Brand Loyalty for Hotels and Airbnb. *Journal of Travel Research, 59*(1), 173-189.

Intrinsic motivation

Definition: Intrinsic motivation is described as an inherent tendency that individuals engage in activities due to their inner interests, pleasure and satisfaction, like a self-rewarding.

> **Source:** Chang, Y., Hou, R.-J., Wang, K., Cui, A. P. & Zhang, C.-B. (2020). Effects of intrinsic and extrinsic motivation on social loafing in online travel communities. *Computers in Human Behavior, 109*, 106360.

Intuitive decision-making

Definition: Intuitive decision-making is an unconscious process involving holistic associations, although there is no agreement regarding whether intuition is derived from experience or from immature preferences.

> **Source:** Carah, N. & Brodmerkel, S. (2020). Critical perspectives on brand culture in the era of participatory and algorithmic media. *Sociology Compass, 14*(2), e12752.

Involvement

Definition (1): Involvement is defined as the perception of the correlation of participation based on internal needs, values, and interests.

> **Source:** McClure, C. & Seock, Y.-K. (2020). The role of involvement: Investigating the effect of brand's social media pages on consumer purchase intention. *Journal of Retailing and Consumer Services, 53*, 101975.

Definition (2): Involvement refers to a state of arousal, motivation, or intense interest in a product, activity, or object there are at least two dimensions of involvement: psychological and behavioural.

> **Source:** Kim, S., Kim, S. & Petrick, J. F. (2019). The Effect of Film Nostalgia on Involvement, Familiarity, and Behavioral Intentions. *Journal of Travel Research, 58*(2), 283-297.

Definition (3): Involvement is the perceived relevance of the object (or brand) based on inherent needs, values, and interests. Involvement may be cognitive, affective, and motivational, but not behavioral.

Source: Harrigan, P., Evers, U., Miles, M. P. & Daly, T. (2018). Customer engagement and the relationship between involvement, engagement, self-brand connection and brand usage intent. *Journal of Business Research, 88*, 388-396.

Kinematic brand logo

Definition: Kinematic logo is a logo with a motion without a force applied.

Source: Baxter, S. M. & Ilicic, J. (2018). May the force drag your dynamic logo: The brand work-energy effect. *International Journal of Research in Marketing, 35*(3), 509-523.

Knowledge

Definition: Knowledge is viewed as the extent to which the stakeholder is informed and experienced with a brand.

Source: Merz, M. A., Zarantonello, L. & Grappi, S. (2018). How valuable are your customers in the brand value co-creation process? The development of a Customer Co-Creation Value (CCCV) scale. *Journal of Business Research, 82*, 79-89.

Legitimacy

Definition: Legitimacy can be defined as the actions of an entity (or brand) are desirable, proper, or appropriate within some socially constructed system of norms, values, beliefs, and definitions.

Source: Hu, M., Qiu, P., Wan, F. & Stillman, T. (2018). Love or hate, depends on who's saying it: How legitimacy of brand rejection alters brand preferences. *Journal of Business Research, 90*, 164-170.

Lifetime value metric

Definition: The lifetime value metric is based on customer transactions over two trading cycles—the last (or current) cycle and the next one.

Source: Ramaswami, S. N. & Arunachalam, S. (2016). Divided attitudinal loyalty and customer value: role of dealers in an indirect channel. *Journal of the Academy of Marketing Science, 44*(6), 770-790.

Local brands

Definition: Local brands have been defined as brands that are available only within a limited geographic region or brands originating from the consumer's home country.

Source: Sichtmann, C., Davvetas, V. & Diamantopoulos, A. (2019). The relational value of perceived brand globalness and localness. *Journal of Business Research, 104*, 597-613.

Longitudinal consistency

Definition: Longitudinal consistency is defined as the extent to which consumers perceive that the brand has not changed and offer evidence that consistency is a sub-dimension of stability in the context of celebrity authenticity.

> **Source:** Moulard, J. G., Raggio, R. D. & Folse, J. A. G. (2016). Brand Authenticity: Testing the Antecedents and Outcomes of Brand Management's Passion for its Products. *Psychology & Marketing*, *33*(6), 421-436.

Loyalty

Definition: Loyalty may be described as a customer's intent or predisposition to buy from the same seller or the same brand again and is a consequence of the belief that the value received from the said seller or brand is great.

> **Source:** Agyei, J., Sun, S., Abrokwah, E., Penney, E. K. & Ofori-Boafo, R. (2020). Influence of Trust on Customer Engagement: Empirical Evidence From the Insurance Industry in Ghana. *SAGE Open*, *10*(1), 2158244019899104.

Luxury brand

Definition (1): A luxury brand signs products or services that consumers perceive to be high quality, offer authentic value via desired benefits, whether functional or emotional and have a prestigious image within the market, built on qualities such as artisans.

> **Source:** Merk, M. & Michel, G. (2019). The dark side of salesperson brand identification in the luxury sector: When brand orientation generates management issues and negative customer perception. *Journal of Business Research*, *102*, 339-352.

Definition (2): Luxury brand is a brand with a premium quality and/or an esthetically appealing design that are exclusive, which implies expensiveness and/or rarity.

> **Source:** Schade, M., Hegner, S., Horstmann, F. & Brinkmann, N. (2016). The impact of attitude functions on luxury brand consumption: An age-based group comparison. *Journal of Business Research*, *69*(1), 314-322.

Definition (3): Luxury brands are defined as high quality, expensive, and non-essential products and services that appear to be rare, exclusive, prestigious, and authentic and offer high levels of symbolic and emotional/hedonic values.

> **Source:** Lee, J. E. & Watkins, B. (2016). YouTube vloggers' influence on consumer luxury brand perceptions and intentions. *Journal of Business Research*, *69*(12), 5753-5760.

Luxury consumption tendency

Definition: Luxury consumption tendency is the extent of an individual's propensity toward the consumption of unique and expensive products/services, with their symbolic meanings that are arbitrarily desired for some reason.

> **Source:** Dogan, V., Ozkara, B. Y. & Dogan, M. (2020). Luxury Consumption Tendency: Conceptualization, Scale Development and Validation. *Current Psychology*, 39(3), 934-952.

Luxury product

Definition: Luxury product can be defined as a work of art designed for an exclusive market and is a branded product that is conspicuous, unique, and carefully crafted.

> **Source:** Salehzadeh, R. & Pool, J. K. (2017). Brand Attitude and Perceived Value and Purchase Intention toward Global Luxury Brands. *Journal of International Consumer Marketing*, 29(2), 74-82.

Market orientation

Definition: Market orientation is defined as an organisational culture that creates necessary behaviours for creating superior value for consumers. Market orientation also refers to the company mindset about consumer need.

> **Source:** Bridson, K. C. & Evans, J. (2018). Brand compass: charting a course to improve firm performance. *Journal of Strategic Marketing*, 26(2), 174-187.

Market presence

Definition: Market presence is the ubiquity of a brand in the market influenced by consumer attitudes or branding activities.

> **Source:** Krautz, C. (2017). A Cross-Cultural Study of Collective Brand Perceptions Within The Brand Equity Framework. *Journal of Marketing Theory and Practice*, 25(3), 274-290.

Materialism

Definition: Materialism is a set of centrally held beliefs about the importance of possessions in one's life and it is also considered as an orientation which views material goods and money as being important for personal happiness and social progress.

> **Source:** Bıçakcıoğlu, N., Ögel, İ. Y. & İlter, B. (2017). Brand jealousy and willingness to pay premium: The mediating role of materialism. *Journal of Brand Management*, 24(1), 33-48.

Model TTF - task-technology fit Model

Definition: Task-technology fit model is defined as the match between the requirements of a task and the capabilities of the technology designed to support task accomplishment.

> **Source:** Tang, Z., Chen, L. & Gillenson, M. L. (2019). Understanding brand fan page followers' discontinuance motivations: A mixed-method study. *Information & Management, 56*(1), 94-108.

Moral identity

Definition: Moral identity is defined as a mental representation that a consumer may hold about his or her moral character.

> **Source:** Wong, T. C., Haddoud Mohamed, Y., Kwok, Y. K. & He, H. (2018). Examining the key determinants towards online pro-brand and anti-brand community citizenship behaviours: A two-stage approach. *Industrial Management & Data Systems, 118*(4), 850-

Narcissism

Definition: Narcissism translates into excessive and sometimes disproportionate attention paid to one's body as an object of fantasy and desire. Narcissistic people generally use their bodies as a social showcase of self-expression.

> **Source:** Korai, B. (2017). Determinants of African Women's Brand Sensitivity Toward Cosmetics. *Journal of International Consumer Marketing, 29*(4), 250-264.

Narrative fidelity

Definition: Narrative fidelity are described as the degree to which the story accords with the logic of good reasons and reflects internalized standards of how people ought to act.

> **Source:** Hamby, A., Brinberg, D. & Daniloski, K. (2019). It's about our values: How founder's stories influence brand authenticity. *Psychology & Marketing, 36*(11), 1014-1026.

Native advertising

Definition: Native advertising is defined as the practice by which a marketer borrows from the credibility of a content publisher by presenting paid content with a format and location that matches the publisher's original content.

> **Source:** Hayes, J. L., Golan, G., Britt, B. & Applequist, J. (2020). How advertising relevance and consumer–Brand relationship strength limit disclosure effects of native ads on Twitter. *International Journal of Advertising, 39*(1), 131-165.

Negative word of mouth

Definition: Negative word of mouth is defined as an intense and broadly communicated negative storyline about the brand.

> **Source:** Nadeau, J., Rutter, R. & Lettice, F. (2020). Social media responses and brand personality in product and moral harm crises: why waste a good crisis? *Journal of Marketing Management, 36*(11-12), 1031-1054.

Non-verbal communication

Definition: Non-verbal communication is defined as the meaning communicated by intended or unintended gestures of the body and space.

> **Source:** Karanges, E., Johnston, K. A., Lings, I. & Beatson, A. T. (2018). Brand signalling: An antecedent of employee brand understanding. *Journal of Brand Management, 25*(3), 235-249.

Nostalgia

Definition: Nostalgia is defined as a longing for the past, a yearning for yesterday, or a fondness for possessions and activities associated with days of yore.

> **Source:** Sichtmann, C., Davvetas, V. & Diamantopoulos, A. (2019). The relational value of perceived brand globalness and localness. *Journal of Business Research, 104*, 597-613.

Omnichannel

Definition: Omnichannel is defined as the synergetic management of the numerous available channels and customer touchpoints, in such a way that the customer experience across channels and the performance over channels is optimized.

> **Source:** Hickman, E., Kharouf, H. & Sekhon, H. (2020). An omnichannel approach to retailing: demystifying and identifying the factors influencing an omnichannel experience. *The International Review of Retail, Distribution and Consumer Research, 30*(3), 266-

Online brand community

Definition: Online brand community is an aggregation of self-selected people who share a common interest and communicate through computer-mediated mechanism.

> **Source:** Chang, A., Hsieh Sara, H. & Tseng Timmy, H. (2013). Online brand community response to negative brand events: the role of group eWOM. *Internet Research, 23*(4), 486-506.

Openness to experience

Definition: Openness to experience are associated with people with high levels of the openness trait are imaginative, daring and creative.

> **Source:** Vashist, D. (2018). Effect of product involvement and brand prominence on advergamers' brand recall and brand attitude in an emerging market context. *Asia Pacific Journal of Marketing and Logistics*, 30(1), 43-61.

Opinion leaders

Definition: Opinion leaders are consumers who have the ability to trigger feedback, spark conversation within a community, or even shape the way that other members of a group 'talk' about a topic.

> **Source:** Kelley James, B. & Alden Dana, L. (2016). Online brand community: through the eyes of Self-Determination Theory. *Internet Research*, 26(4), 790-808.

Original attribute

Definition: Original attribute is the brand differentiating itself from competitors through a novel approach to brand positioning.

> **Source:** Portal, S., Abratt, R. & Bendixen, M. (2018). Building a human brand: Brand anthropomorphism unravelled. *Business Horizons*, 61(3), 367-374.

Original brand

Definition: Original brand is associated to the brands with a tendency to be diferent, creative and to do things that not been done before.

> **Source:** Warren, C., Batra, R., Loureiro, S. M. C. & Bagozzi, R. P. (2019). Brand Coolness. *Journal of Marketing*, 83(5), 36-56.

Overall brand equity

Definition: Overall brand equity is defined as the value added to the branded product relative to the unbranded product.

> **Source:** Zhang, J., Jiang, Y., Shabbir, R. & Zhu, M. (2016). How brand orientation impacts B2B service brand equity? An empirical study among Chinese firms. *Journal of Business & Industrial Marketing*, 31(1), 83-98.

Para-social interaction

Definition: Para-social interaction is an illusionary experience, such that consumers interact with personas (i.e., mediated representations of presenters, celebrities, or characters) as if they are present and engaged in a reciprocal relationship.

> **Source:** Lee, J. E. & Watkins, B. (2016). YouTube vloggers' influence on consumer luxury brand perceptions and intentions. *Journal of Business Research*, 69(12), 5753-5760.

Passion
Definition: Passion is the extent to which the stakeholder has extremely positive feelings toward the brand.

> **Source:** Merz, M. A., Zarantonello, L. & Grappi, S. (2018). How valuable are your customers in the brand value co-creation process? The development of a Customer Co-Creation Value (CCCV) scale. *Journal of Business Research, 82,* 79-89.

Perceived behavioural
Definition: Perceived behavioral control is described as the perceived ease or difficulty of performing the behavior.

> **Source:** Bianchi, C., Milberg, S. & Cúneo, A. (2017). Understanding travelers' intentions to visit a short versus long-haul emerging vacation destination: The case of Chile. *Tourism Management, 59,* 312-324.

Perceived brand globalness
Definition: Perceived brand globalness refers to consumers' beliefs that a "brand is marketed in multiple countries and is generally recognized as global in these countries.

> **Source:** Mandler, T., Bartsch, F. & Han, C. M. (2020). Brand credibility and marketplace globalization: The role of perceived brand globalness and localness. *Journal of International Business Studies.*

Perceived brand localness
Definition: Perceived brand localness refers to consumers' perceptions that "a brand symbolizes the values, needs, and aspirations of the members of the local country" as the "degree to which a brand symbolizes the values, needs, and aspirations of the members.

> **Source:** Mandler, T., Bartsch, F. & Han, C. M. (2020). Brand credibility and marketplace globalization: The role of perceived brand globalness and localness. *Journal of International Business Studies.*

Perceived brand quality
Definition: Perceived brand quality is defined as the consumer's judgment about a product's overall excellence or superiority.

> **Source:** Bazi, S., Filieri, R. & Gorton, M. (2020). Customers' motivation to engage with luxury brands on social media. *Journal of Business Research, 112,* 223-235.

Perceived fit
Definition: Perceived fit is defined as the number of shared associations between the brand and the extension.

> **Source:** Pourazad, N., Stocchi, L. & Pare, V. (2019). Brand attribute associations, emotional consumer-brand relationship and evaluation of brand extensions. *Australasian Marketing Journal (AMJ), 27*(4), 249-260.

Perceived playfulness

Definition: Perceived playfulness refers to the intrinsic motivation that focusses on the process of fun, creativity, enjoyment and pleasure by engaging in absorbing interactions.

> **Source:** Lee Crystal, T. & Hsieh Sara, H. (2019). Engaging consumers in mobile instant messaging: the role of cute branded emoticons. *Journal of Product & Brand Management, 28*(7), 849-863.

Perceived privacy

Definition: Perceived privacy refers to the perceptions that legal requirements and good practices exist to manage personal data.

> **Source:** Kim, Y. & Peterson, R. A. (2017). A Meta-analysis of Online Trust Relationships in E-commerce. *Journal of Interactive Marketing, 38*, 44-54.

Perceived quality

Definition (1): Perceived quality is generally defined as the customer's judgment of the overall excellence, esteem, or superiority of a brand (with respect to its intended purposes) relative to alternative brand(s).

> **Source:** Filieri, R., Lin, Z., D'Antone, S. & Chatzopoulou, E. (2019). A cultural approach to brand equity: the role of brand mianzi and brand popularity in China. *Journal of Brand Management, 26*(4), 376-394.

Definition (2): Perceived quality is defined as consumer's overall evaluation of a specific service firm that results from comparing that firm's performance with the customer's general expectations of how firms in that industry should perform.

> **Source:** Han, H., Nguyen, H. N., Song, H., Chua, B.-L., Lee, S. & Kim, W. (2018). Drivers of brand loyalty in the chain coffee shop industry. *International Journal of Hospitality Management, 72*, 86-97.

Definition (3): Perceived quality is defined as the perception of the overall quality or superiority of a product or service relative to relevant alternatives and with respect to its intended purpose.

> **Source:** Cano Guervos, R. A., Frías Jamilena, D. M., Polo Peña, A. I. & Chica Olmo, J. (2020). Influence of Tourist Geographical Context on Customer-Based Destination Brand Equity: An Empirical Analysis. *Journal of Travel Research, 59*(1), 107-119.

Perceived risk

Definition (1): Perceived risk is defined as a consumer's belief about the potential uncertain negative outcomes from the online transaction that must be present for trust to emerge such that trust would mitigate the uncertainties and risks.

>**Source:** Kim, Y. & Peterson, R. A. (2017). A Meta-analysis of Online Trust Relationships in E-commerce. *Journal of Interactive Marketing*, 38, 44-54.

Definition (2): perceived risk is associated to the consumers' perceptions of uncertainty and adverse consequence of buying a product or service. The risks can be categorized into various types: financial, time, psychological, social, and performance risk.

>**Source:** Trivedi, J. (2019). Examining the Customer Experience of Using Banking Chatbots and Its Impact on Brand Love: The Moderating Role of Perceived Risk. *Journal of Internet Commerce*, 18(1), 91-111.

Perceived security

Definition: Perceived security refers to the perception that technical guarantees involving legal requirements and good practices related to privacy will be met.

>**Source:** Kim, Y. & Peterson, R. A. (2017). A Meta-analysis of Online Trust Relationships in E-commerce. *Journal of Interactive Marketing*, 38, 44-54.

Perceived service quality

Definition: Perceived service quality is the consumer's subjective evaluation of the interaction quality with a website and how well the service needs have been met

>**Source:** Kim, Y. & Peterson, R. A. (2017). A Meta-analysis of Online Trust Relationships in E-commerce. *Journal of Interactive Marketing*, 38, 44-54.

Perceived strength of brand origin

Definition: Perceived strength of brand origin is defined as a consumer's holistic perception of congruence between brand image and country image.

>**Source:** Siew, S.-W., Minor, M. S. & Felix, R. (2018). The influence of perceived strength of brand origin on willingness to pay more for luxury goods. *Journal of Brand Management*, 25(6), 591-605.

Perceived system quality

Definition: Perceived system quality refers to the technical and functional characteristics of an information system pertaining to reliability, flexibility, accessibility, and timeliness.

Source: Kim, Y. & Peterson, R. A. (2017). A Meta-analysis of Online Trust Relationships in E-commerce. *Journal of Interactive Marketing, 38*, 44-54.

Perceived usefulness

Definition: Perceived usefulness refers to the degree to which consumers believe that a particular technology will facilitate the transaction process.

Source: Kim, Y. & Peterson, R. A. (2017). A Meta-analysis of Online Trust Relationships in E-commerce. *Journal of Interactive Marketing, 38*, 44-54.

Perceived value

Definition (1): Perceived value is the consumer's overall assessment of the utility of a product based on perceptions of what is received and what is given and represents an overall estimation of a choice object.

Source: Zhao, H., Su, C. & Hua, Z. (2016). Investigating continuance intention to follow a brand micro-blog:Perceived value and social identification. *Information Development, 32*(5), 1428-1441.

Definition (2): Perceived value of a service relates to the benefits customers believe they receive relative to the costs associated with its consumption, and is an overall evaluation of a service's utility, based on customers' perceptions.

Source: Cano Guervos, R. A., Frías Jamilena, D. M., Polo Peña, A. I. & Chica Olmo, J. (2020). Influence of Tourist Geographical Context on Customer-Based Destination Brand Equity: An Empirical Analysis. *Journal of Travel Research, 59*(1), 107-119.

Definition (3): Perceived value is commonly defined as a ratio or trade-off of total benefits received to total sacrifices.

Source: González-Mansilla, Ó., Berenguer-Contrí, G. & Serra-Cantallops, A. (2019). The impact of value co-creation on hotel brand equity and customer satisfaction. *Tourism Management, 75*, 51-65.

Performance Risk

Definition: Performance risk is similar to the overall risk involved in using a product or service, and refers to the perceived risk of a product or service not delivering as expected or failing in totality.

Source: Trivedi, J. (2019). Examining the Customer Experience of Using Banking Chatbots and Its Impact on Brand Love: The Moderating Role of Perceived Risk. *Journal of Internet Commerce, 18*(1), 91-111.

Personal control

Definition: Personal control refers to the belief that one is capable of obtaining desired outcomes and achieving goals, arises from the perception of clear contingencies between actions and outcomes.

> **Source:** Khenfer, J. & Cuny, C. (2020). Brand preference in the face of control loss and service failure: The role of the sound of brands. *Journal of Retailing and Consumer Services*, 55, 102132.

Persuasion knowledge

Definition: Persuasion knowledge refers to consumers' perception and beliefs about marketers' motives and manipulative intents.

> **Source:** Qin, Y., Wen, N., and Dou, W. (2016) Effects of perceptual and conceptual similarities on consumers' evaluations of copycat brand names. J. Consumer Behaviour., 15: 117– 125

Philanthropic sponsorship

Definition: Philanthropic sponsorship implies assistance for a cultural or social cause with no commercial benefits expected.

> **Source:** Shin, H., Lee, H. & Perdue, R. R. (2018). The congruity effects of commercial brand sponsorship in a regional event. *Tourism Management*, 67, 168-179.

Place brand attachment

Definition: Place brand attachment involves an interplay of affect and emotions, knowledge and beliefs, and behaviors and actions.

> **Source:** Chen, N. & Dwyer, L. (2018). Residents' Place Satisfaction and Place Attachment on Destination Brand-Building Behaviors: Conceptual and Empirical Differentiation. *Journal of Travel Research*, 57(8), 1026-1041.

Place brand

Definition: Place brand is a network of associations in the consumers' mind based on the visual, verbal and behavioural expression of a place, which is embodied through the aims, communication, values and the general culture of the place's stakeholders.

> **Source:** Rowley, J. & Hanna, S. (2020). Branding destinations: symbolic and narrative representations and co-branding. *Journal of Brand Management*, 27(3), 328-338.

Place satisfaction

Definition: Place satisfaction is defined as residents' subjective evaluation of benefits across the rich bundle of goods and services.

> Source: Chen, N. & Dwyer, L. (2018). Residents' Place Satisfaction and Place Attachment on Destination Brand-Building Behaviors: Conceptual and Empirical Differentiation. *Journal of Travel Research, 57*(8), 1026-1041.

Political brand

Definition: Political brand has been regarded as analogous to commercial brand typologies that facilitate the development of increased knowledge of brand and voter behavior and align the political brand with consumers' requirements to achieve desired results.

> Source: Ahmed, M. A., Lodhi, S. A. & Ahmad, Z. (2017). Political Brand Equity Model: The Integration of Political Brands in Voter Choice. *Journal of Political Marketing, 16*(2), 147-179.

Popular brand

Definition: Popular brand is a brand which is fashionable, trendy and likely by most people.

> Source: Warren, C., Batra, R., Loureiro, S. M. C. & Bagozzi, R. P. (2019). Brand Coolness. *Journal of Marketing, 83*(5), 36-56.

Power

Definition: Power is typically defined as the ability to control valued resources and the capacity to influence the behavior of others.

> Source: Charlton, A. B. & Cornwell, T. B. (2019). Authenticity in horizontal marketing partnerships: A better measure of brand compatibility. *Journal of Business Research, 100*, 279-298.

Presented brand

Definition: Presented brand is defined as the brand message that a company conceptualizes and disseminates.

> Source: Zhang, J., Jiang, Y., Shabbir, R. & Zhu, M. (2016). How brand orientation impacts B2B service brand equity? An empirical study among Chinese firms. *Journal of Business & Industrial Marketing, 31*(1), 83-98.

Price consciousness

Definition: Price consciousness is defined as finding the best value, buying at sale prices or the lowest price choice.

> Source: Wolak, A., Fijorek, K., Zając, G. & Kumbár, V. (2019). What Drives Consumers in Poland and the Czech Republic When Choosing Engine Oil Brand? *Entrepreneurial Business and Economics Review, 7*, 165-184.

Private labels

Definition: Private labels are a retailer's own brands and allow the retailer to differentiate its offerings from those of competing brands and retailers.

> **Source:** Molinillo, S., Japutra, A., Nguyen, B. & Chen Cheng-Hao, S. (2017). Responsible brands vs active brands? An examination of brand personality on brand awareness, brand trust, and brand loyalty. *Marketing Intelligence & Planning*, 35(2), 166-179.

Process innovation

Definition: Process innovation refers to the firms' development of new products through new technology or new production systems.

> **Source:** Zameer, H., Wang, Y. & Yasmeen, H. (2019). Transformation of firm innovation activities into brand effect. *Marketing Intelligence & Planning*, 37(2), 226-240.

Processing fluency

Definition: Processing fluency is defined as the ease with which individuals process information, influences human behavior.

> **Source:** Huang, R., Ha, S. & Kim, S.-H. (2018). Narrative persuasion in social media: an empirical study of luxury brand advertising. *Journal of Research in Interactive Marketing*, 12(3), 274-292.

Product category involvement

Definition: Product-category involvement has been defined as a person's perceived relevance of the object based on inherent needs, values, and interest.

> **Source:** Vashist, D. (2018). Effect of product involvement and brand prominence on advergamers' brand recall and brand attitude in an emerging market context. *Asia Pacific Journal of Marketing and Logistics*, 30(1), 43-61.

Product design appeal

Definition: Product design appeal refers to the extent to which the product design is perceived as beautiful, stunning, gorgeous, hence "the consumer's perception of attractiveness and pleasure from its appearance.

> **Source:** Bazi, S., Filieri, R. & Gorton, M. (2020). Customers' motivation to engage with luxury brands on social media. *Journal of Business Research*, 112, 223-235.

Product involvement's efficacy

Definition: Product involvement's efficacy is defined as consumers' feelings of interest and enthusiasm toward product categories.

Source: Lee Crystal, T. & Hsieh Sara, H. (2019). Engaging consumers in mobile instant messaging: the role of cute branded emoticons. *Journal of Product & Brand Management, 28*(7), 849-863.

Product placement

Definition: Product placement is associated to the inclusion of a brand name, product, or logo within a scripted medium and is ostensibly integrated with this medium.

Source: Vashist, D. (2018). Effect of product involvement and brand prominence on advergamers' brand recall and brand attitude in an emerging market context. *Asia Pacific Journal of Marketing and Logistics, 30*(1), 43-61.

Product-harm crisis

Definition: Product-harm crisis is defined as a discrete event in which products are found to be defective and therefore dangerous to at least part of the product's customer base.

Source: Khamitov, M., Grégoire, Y. & Suri, A. (2020). A systematic review of brand transgression, service failure recovery and product-harm crisis: integration and guiding insights. *Journal of the Academy of Marketing Science, 48*(3), 519-542.

Psychological involvement

Definition: Psychological involvement indicates an individual's degree of attitudinal attachment with an activity, whereas behavioral involvement refers to the intensity of effort or time expended in the processes of information searching, participation, and purchasing.

Source: Kim, S., Kim, S. & Petrick, J. F. (2019). The Effect of Film Nostalgia on Involvement, Familiarity, and Behavioral Intentions. *Journal of Travel Research, 58*(2), 283-297.

Psychological well-being

Definition: Psychological well-being is based on the theory of eudaimonia that defines well-being in terms of the extent to which a person is fully functioning and capable of realizing his/her true potential.

Source: Jian, Y., Zhou, Z. & Zhou, N. (2019). Brand cultural symbolism, brand authenticity, and consumer well-being: the moderating role of cultural involvement. *Journal of Product & Brand Management, 28*(4), 529-539.

Public-based evaluation

Definition: Public-based evaluation is defined as brand evaluations under social influences.

Source: Sugitani, Y. (2018). The Effect of Self- and Public-Based Evaluations on Brand Purchasing: The Interplay of Independent and Interdependent Self-Construal. *Journal of International Consumer Marketing, 30*(4), 235-243.

Purchase intention

Definition (1): Purchase intention is defined as the potential transaction behavior and purchase likelihood of consumers exhibited after evaluating a product.

> **Source:** Min, J. H. J., Chang, H. J. J., Jai, T.-M. C. & Ziegler, M. (2019). The effects of celebrity-brand congruence and publicity on consumer attitudes and buying behavior. *Fashion and Textiles*, 6(1), 10.

Definition (2): Purchase intention is the consumer's volitional commitment to purchase a product/service from an online vendor.

> **Source:** Kim, Y. & Peterson, R. A. (2017). A Meta-analysis of Online Trust Relationships in E-commerce. *Journal of Interactive Marketing*, 38, 44-54.

Definition (3): Purchase intention refers to the combination of consumers' interest in a brand or a product and the likelihood of purchasing these items. It is strongly related to the attitude and preference toward a particular brand or a product.

> **Source:** Dabbous, A. & Barakat, K. A. (2020). Bridging the online offline gap: Assessing the impact of brands' social network content quality on brand awareness and purchase intention. *Journal of Retailing and Consumer Services*, 53, 101966.

Purchase involvement

Definition: Purchase involvement is the level of interest individuals show for an object depending on their needs, values, and motivations.

> **Source:** Korai, B. (2017). Determinants of African Women's Brand Sensitivity Toward Cosmetics. *Journal of International Consumer Marketing*, 29(4), 250-264.

Quality commitment

Definition: Quality commitment reflects a firm's ongoing endeavour and promise to consumers to continue making a product to the same exacting standards (or better).

> **Source:** Napoli, J., Dickinson-Delaporte, S. & Beverland, M. B. (2016). The brand authenticity continuum: strategic approaches for building value. *Journal of Marketing Management*, 32(13-14), 1201-1229.

Rational decision making

Definition: Rational decision making is the extent to which the decision process involves collecting information relevant to the decision and the reliance upon analysis of this information when making the choice.

> **Source:** Carah, N. & Brodmerkel, S. (2020). Critical perspectives on brand culture in the era of participatory and algorithmic media. *Sociology Compass, 14*(2), e12752.

Rebellious brand
Definition: Rebellious brand is a tendency to oppose, fight, subvert or combat conventions and social norms.

> **Source:** Warren, C., Batra, R., Loureiro, S. M. C. & Bagozzi, R. P. (2019). Brand Coolness. *Journal of Marketing, 83*(5), 36-56.

Relatedness
Definition: Relatedness is also referred to as connectedness or belonging.

> **Source:** Hsieh, S. H. & Chang, A. (2016). The Psychological Mechanism of Brand Co-creation Engagement. *Journal of Interactive Marketing, 33*, 13-26.

Relational brand engagement platforms
Definition: Relational brand engagement platforms entail assemblage systems designed around enterprise activities such as connecting with customers, employees, partners, or any other stakeholders, innovating/marketing offerings and customer service/support.

> **Source:** Ramaswamy, V. & Ozcan, K. (2016). Brand value co-creation in a digitalized world: An integrative framework and research implications. *International Journal of Research in Marketing, 33*(1), 93-106.

Relationship commitment
Definition: Relationship commitment is defined as a notion consisting of developed cooperative sentiments, strong preference for existing partners and propensity for relation continuity.

> **Source:** Han, H., Nguyen, H. N., Song, H., Chua, B.-L., Lee, S. & Kim, W. (2018). Drivers of brand loyalty in the chain coffee shop industry. *International Journal of Hospitality Management, 72*, 86-97.

Relationship equity
Definition: Relationship equity refers to the customer's view of the strength of the relationship between the customer and the firm.

> **Source:** Gao, L., Melero-Polo, I. & Sese, F. J. (2020). Customer Equity Drivers, Customer Experience Quality, and Customer Profitability in Banking Services: The Moderating Role of Social Influence. *Journal of Service Research, 23*(2), 174-193.

Religion
Definition: Religion is an organized system of beliefs, practices, rituals and

symbols designed to facilitate closeness to the sacred or transcendent (God, higher power, or ultimate truth/reality), and to foster an understanding of one's relation and responsibility to others.

> **Source:** Hwang, C. & Kim, T. H. (2020) Muslim Women's Purchasing Behaviors Toward Modest Activewear in the United States. *Clothing and Textiles Research Journal*, 0887302X20926573.

Repurchase intention

Definition: Repurchase intention represents a loyalty outcome of customer brand relationships. is defined as the tendency of a customer to repurchase the same brand, select a focal brand as a primary choice as well as loyalty to the focal brand.

> **Source:** Nyadzayo, M. W., Leckie, C. & Johnson, L. W. (2020). The impact of relational drivers on customer brand engagement and brand outcomes. *Journal of Brand Management*, 27(5), 561-578.

Responsible brand personality

Definition: Responsibility brand personality includes three personality traits: down to earth, stable, and responsible.

> **Source:** Molinillo, S., Japutra, A., Nguyen, B. & Chen Cheng-Hao, S. (2017). Responsible brands vs active brands? An examination of brand personality on brand awareness, brand trust, and brand loyalty. *Marketing Intelligence & Planning*, 35(2), 166-179.

Retailer equity

Definition: Retailer equity is defined as a set of brand assets and liabilities linked to a store brand (e.g., Wal-Mart), its name and symbol, that adds to or subtracts from the perceived value of the store brand by its consumers.

> **Source:** Londoño, J. C., Elms, J. & Davies, K. (2016). Conceptualising and measuring consumer-based brand–retailer–channel equity. *Journal of Retailing and Consumer Services*, 29, 70-81.

Retailer reliability

Definition: Retailer reliability is defined as the willingness of the average consumer to rely on the ability of the retailer to perform its function. Reliability is contingent on the perceived ability of the retailer.

> **Source:** Massara, F., Scarpi, D., Melara, R. D. & Porcheddu, D. (2018). Affect transfer from national brands to store brands in multi-brand stores. *Journal of Retailing and Consumer Services*, 45, 103-110.

Risk aversion

Definition: Risk aversion is defined as the extent to which people feel threatened by ambiguous situations, and have created beliefs and institutions that try to avoid these.

> **Source:** Alhosseini Almodarresi Seyed, M. & Rasty, F. (2019). The moderating effect of emotion regulation on the relationship between risk aversion and brand sensitivity. *Journal of Product & Brand Management, 28*(1), 95-103.

Role theory

Definition: Role theory posits that successful social interaction depends on whether relationship partners behave appropriately according to their specific social role in a relationship.

> **Source:** Gretry, A., Horváth, C., Belei, N. & van Riel, A. C. R. (2017). "Don't pretend to be my friend!" When an informal brand communication style backfires on social media. *Journal of Business Research, 74,* 77-89.

Satisfaction

Definition: Satisfaction is the outcome of the customer's view of value against the quality of services perceived, comparative to the cost.

> **Source:** Rashid, R. M., Rashid, Q. u. A., Nawaz, M. A. & Akhtar, S. (2019). Young Chinese consumers' brand perception; the role of mianzi as moderator. *Journal of Public Affairs, 19*(4), e1930.

Schema congruity

Definition: A schema congruity is a stored structure of cognitive knowledge that represents specific knowledge about various stimuli, including the attributes and their relations.

> **Source:** Wang, S. S., Lin, Y.-C. & Liang, T.-P. (2018). Posts that attract millions of fans: The effect of brand-post congruence. *Electronic Commerce Research and Applications, 28,* 73-85.

Secret affairs with brands

Definition: Secret affairs with brands are defined as privately held relationships that allow consumers to indulge brand consumption and feel playful.

> **Source:** Dimitriu, R. & Guesalaga, R. (2017). Consumers' Social Media Brand Behaviors: Uncovering Underlying Motivators and Deriving Meaningful Consumer Segments. *Psychology & Marketing, 34*(5), 580-592

Self-based evaluation

Definition: Self-based evaluation refers to the personal evaluation derived from the relationship between the brand and the self.

> **Source:** Sugitani, Y. (2018). The Effect of Self- and Public-Based Evaluations on Brand Purchasing: The Interplay of Independent and Interdependent Self-Construal. *Journal of International Consumer Marketing, 30*(4), 235-243.

Self congruence

Definition (1): Self brand congruence is associated a subjective experience of "fit" or "consistency" with the brand.

>Source: Mandal, S. (2020). Employing autobiographical memory perspective to influence self-congruence and brand preference. *Journal of Consumer Behaviour, 19*(5), 481-492.

Definition: Actual and ideal self-congruence refer to the consumer's self-concept and are based on the perceived fit of the communicated brand image with the consumer's actual self-image and ideal self-image, respectively.

>Source: Fritz, K., Schoenmueller, V. & Bruhn, M. (2017). Authenticity in branding – exploring antecedents and consequences of brand authenticity. *European Journal of Marketing, 51*(2), 324-348.

Self expressive brand

Definition: Self-expressive brand can be defined as 'a consumer's perception of the degree to which the specific brand reflects one's inner self'.

>Source: Leckie, C., Nyadzayo, M. W. & Johnson, L. W. (2016). Antecedents of consumer brand engagement and brand loyalty. *Journal of Marketing Management, 32*(5-6), 558-578.

Self-acceptance'

Definition: Self-acceptance' denotes a class of psychological phenomena that involves taking a tendentiously positive view of oneself and allows a person to develop a favourable self-view.

>Source: Panda, T. K., Kumar, A., Jakhar, S., Luthra, S., Garza-Reyes, J. A., Kazancoglu, I. & Nayak, S. S. (2020). Social and environmental sustainability model on consumers' altruism, green purchase intention, green brand loyalty and evangelism. *Journal of Cleaner*

Self-brand connection

Definition (1): Self-brand connection is the operationalization of the self-congruity mechanism in a framework in which the union between the consumer's identity and the brand's personality or image is determined.

>Source: Moliner Miguel, Á., Monferrer-Tirado, D. & Estrada-Guillén, M. (2018). Consequences of customer engagement and customer self-brand connection. *Journal of Services Marketing, 32*(4), 387-399.

Definition (2): Self-brand connection refers to the extent to which individuals have incorporated brands into their self-concept and is a significant antecedent of brand performance.

>Source: Sugitani, Y. (2018). The Effect of Self- and Public-Based Evaluations on Brand

Purchasing: The Interplay of Independent and Interdependent Self-Construal. *Journal of International Consumer Marketing, 30*(4), 235-243.

Self-brand identification

Definition: Self-brand identification is defined as a consumer's 'perceived state of oneness with a brand which implies perceiving, feeling and valuing a psychosomatic connection with the brand.

> **Source:** Pourazad, N., Stocchi, L. & Pare, V. (2019). Brand attribute associations, emotional consumer-brand relationship and evaluation of brand extensions. *Australasian Marketing Journal (AMJ), 27*(4), 249-260.

Self-brand integration

Definition: Self-brand integration is a cognitive merging of the brand and the individual's self so that brand meanings are experienced as the individual's own.

> **Source:** Delgado-Ballester, E., Palazón, M. & Peláez, J. (2019). Anthropomorphized vs objectified brands: which brand version is more loved? *European Journal of Management and Business Economics, 29*(2), 150-165.

Self-branding

Definition: Self-branding, also known as personal branding and it is defined as individuals developing a distinguishing public image for commercial gain and/or cultural capital.

> **Source:** Mann, B. J. S., Parmar, Y. & Ghuman, M. K. A (2020) New Scale to Capture the Multidimensionality of Celebrity Image. *Global Business Review.*

Self-concept

Definition (1): Self concept is defined as the sum of one's thoughts and feelings about oneself pertaining to others, and can be taken in two forms: the actual self and the ideal self.

> **Source:** Zhu, X., Teng, L., Foti, L. & Yuan, Y. (2019). Using self-congruence theory to explain the interaction effects of brand type and celebrity type on consumer attitude formation. *Journal of Business Research, 103,* 301-309.

Definition (2): Self-concept or self-image conceptualize the consumer's sense of self, which essentially denotes the totality of the individual's thoughts and feelings having reference to himself as an object.

> **Source:** Mandal, S. (2020). Employing autobiographical memory perspective to influence self-congruence and brand preference. *Journal of Consumer Behaviour, 19*(5), 481-492.

Self-congruency

Definition: Self-congruency is the congruity between the actual self-image and product image or brand image.

>**Source:** Bazi, S., Filieri, R. & Gorton, M. (2020). Customers' motivation to engage with luxury brands on social media. *Journal of Business Research, 112,* 223-235.

Self-congruity

Definition (1): Self-congruity has been defined as the combination or degree of alignment between the image of the product/brand and the self-concept of the consumer. Self-congruity is a natural extension of the self-concept theory. This theory is multidimensional and it consists of an actual self-congruity, ideal self-congruity, social self-congruity, and ideal social self-congruity

>**Source:** Cano Guervos, R. A., Frías Jamilena, D. M., Polo Peña, A. I. & Chica Olmo, J. (2020). Influence of Tourist Geographical Context on Customer-Based Destination Brand Equity: An Empirical Analysis. *Journal of Travel Research, 59*(1), 107-119.

Definition (2): Self-congruity is the match between consumers 'self-concept and the image or personality of the product, supplier or service.

>**Source:** Moliner Miguel, Á., Monferrer-Tirado, D. & Estrada-Guillén, M. (2018). Consequences of customer engagement and customer self-brand connection. *Journal of Services Marketing, 32*(4), 387-399.

Self-connection

Definition: Self-connection indicates strength through the activation of an individual's identity system, capturing the extent to which the relationship delivers centrally held identity themes or helps to express real and collective selves.

>**Source:** Jeon Jung, O. & Baeck, S. (2016). What drives consumer's responses to brand crisis? The moderating roles of brand associations and brand-customer relationship strength. *Journal of Product & Brand Management, 25*(6), 550-567.

Self-consciousness

Definition: Self-consciousness is a consistent tendency to direct attention inward or forward. Self-consciousness has some facets: private self-consciousness (personal thoughts about the self), public self-consciousness (others' reactions to the self).

>**Source:** Roux, E., Tafani, E. & Vigneron, F. (2017). Values associated with luxury brand consumption and the role of gender. *Journal of Business Research, 71,* 102-113.

Self-consistency

Definition: Self-consistency motives refer to the tendency to behave consistently with the self-image.

Source: Shin, H., Lee, H. & Perdue, R. R. (2018). The congruity effects of commercial brand sponsorship in a regional event. *Tourism Management, 67*, 168-179.

Self-construal theory

Definition: Self-construal theory posits that individuals may construct their specific selves to differentiate themselves from others. Self-construal is a psychological term that describes how individuals perceive, comprehend, and interpret the world.

Source: Pan, L.-Y., Huang, H.-C. & Ko, C.-H. (2020). A prideful posting a day keeps admiring readers awake: voluntary bloggers in a self-construal framework. *Behaviour & Information Technology*, 1-16.

Self-determination theory

Definition: Self-determination theory is one of the leading methods that explicates the dynamics of human needs, motivation and well-being. Self-determination theory divides motivation into categories: intrinsic motivation, extrinsic motivation.

Source: Chang, Y., Hou, R.-J., Wang, K., Cui, A. P. & Zhang, C.-B. (2020). Effects of intrinsic and extrinsic motivation on social loafing in online travel communities. *Computers in Human Behavior, 109*, 106360.

Self-efficacy

Definition: Self-efficacy is defined as self-confidence in one's ability to perform given tasks, reflecting the cognitive and physical ability to effectively use knowledge and skills to complete those tasks.

Source: Shim, C., Kang, S., Kim, I. & Hyun, S. S. (2017). Luxury-cruise travellers' brand community perception and its consequences. *Current Issues in Tourism, 20*(14), 1489-1509.

Self-esteem

Definition (1): Self-esteem motives refer to the tendency to pursue experiences that enhance the self-concept.

Source: Shin, H., Lee, H. & Perdue, R. R. (2018). The congruity effects of commercial brand sponsorship in a regional event. *Tourism Management, 67*, 168-179.

Definition (2): Self-esteem is defined as a spontaneous, natural, and unconscious evaluation of the self that affects unprompted responses to self-relevant stimuli.

Source: Hsieh, S. H. & Chang, A. (2016). The Psychological Mechanism of Brand Co-creation Engagement. *Journal of Interactive Marketing, 33*, 13-26.

Self-reassurance

Definition: Self-reassurance is the tendency to connect with other people to reassure the self of its worth.

> Source: Pan, L.-Y., Huang, H.-C. & Ko, C.-H. (2020). A prideful posting a day keeps admiring readers awake: voluntary bloggers in a self-construal framework. *Behaviour & Information Technology*, 1-16.

Sensory experience

Definition: Sensory experience is related to how consumers respond to a brand's attributes through their sensory organs (i.e., eye, ears, nose, tongue, and skin). The sensory experience can be created through various brand elements that implicitly deliver a brand's content and meaning.

> Source: Kang, J., Kwun, D. J. & Hahm, J. J. (2020). Turning Your Customers into Brand Evangelists: Evidence from Cruise Travelers. *Journal of Quality Assurance in Hospitality & Tourism*, 21(6), 617-643.

Sensory marketing

Definition: Sensory marketing refers to stimulating consumers' senses through marketing tactics, which influences consumers' product evaluations and purchasing behaviour.

> Source: Yoganathan, V., Osburg, V.-S. & Akhtar, P. (2019). Sensory stimulation for sensible consumption: Multisensory marketing for e-tailing of ethical brands. *Journal of Business Research*, 96, 386-396.

Service experience

Definition: Service experience is defined as an actor's subjective response to elements of the service, emerging during the process of purchase and use, or through imagination or memory.

> Source: Trivedi, J. (2019). Examining the Customer Experience of Using Banking Chatbots and Its Impact on Brand Love: The Moderating Role of Perceived Risk. *Journal of Internet Commerce*, 18(1), 91-111.

Service failure

Definition: Service failure is defined as a private service performance that falls below the expectation of one or a few customer(s).

> Source: Khamitov, M., Grégoire, Y. & Suri, A. (2020). A systematic review of brand transgression, service failure recovery and product-harm crisis: integration and guiding insights. *Journal of the Academy of Marketing Science*, 48(3), 519-542.

Service recovery

Definition: Service recovery is defined as all the actions that a firm can take to redress the grievances or loss caused by a service failure.

Source: Khamitov, M., Grégoire, Y. & Suri, A. (2020). A systematic review of brand transgression, service failure recovery and product-harm crisis: integration and guiding insights. *Journal of the Academy of Marketing Science, 48*(3), 519-542.

Shared brand understanding

Definition: Shared brand understanding refers to the ability of all employees to articulate the brand vision, objectives and strategies. For the firm to truly achieve its brand goals then the entire organisation needs to have a clear understanding of the brand vision, its purpose and future.

Source: Bridson, K. C. & Evans, J. (2018). Brand compass: charting a course to improve firm performance. *Journal of Strategic Marketing, 26*(2), 174-187.

Signaling theory

Definition: Signaling theory is one of the dominant paradigms in recruitment research and is typically applied to explain how recruitment activities can influence potential applicants' perceptions of an organization.

Source: Carpentier, M., Van Hoye, G. & Weijters, B. (2019). Attracting applicants through the organization's social media page: Signaling employer brand personality. *Journal of Vocational Behavior, 115*, 103326.

Skills

Definition: Skills is the extent to which the stakeholder is stimulated by the brand in terms of his/her capabilities.

Source: Merz, M. A., Zarantonello, L. & Grappi, S. (2018). How valuable are your customers in the brand value co-creation process? The development of a Customer Co-Creation Value (CCCV) scale. *Journal of Business Research, 82*, 79-89.

Slogans

Definition: Slogans are phrases associated with the brand that can improve the more general attitudes of the brand in at least three ways: through the preparation of specific brand associations; by transferring sympathy from the slogan to the brand, and serving as a memory aid to reinforce the positive brand.

Source: Briggs, E. & Janakiraman, N. (2017). Slogan recall effects on marketplace behaviors: The roles of external search and brand assessment. *Journal of Business Research, 80*, 98-105.

Social Networks Service advertising

Definition: Social networks service advertising entails all forms of advertising, whether explicit (e.g. banner advertising and commercial videos) or implicit (e.g. fan pages or firm-related "tweets") – that are delivered through social networking sites.

Source: Huang, R., Ha, S. & Kim, S.-H. (2018). Narrative persuasion in social media: an empirical study of luxury brand advertising. *Journal of Research in Interactive Marketing*, 12(3), 274-292.

Social benefit

Definition: Social benefit is associated with individuals' needs for recognition and social support.

Source: Source: Pan, L.-Y., Huang, H.-C. & Ko, C.-H. (2020). A prideful posting a day keeps admiring readers awake: voluntary bloggers in a self-construal framework. *Behaviour & Information Technology*, 1-16.

Social identity theory

Definition: Social identity theory suggests that individuals often define their self-concept by perceived membership within a certain social group.

Source: So, K. K. F., Wu, L., Xiong, L. & King, C. (2018). Brand Management in the Era of Social Media: Social Visibility of Consumption and Customer Brand Identification. *Journal of Travel Research*, 57(6), 727-742.

Social influence

Definition: Social influence is conceptualized as the transfer of information from one customer (or a group of customers) to another customer (or group of customers) in a way that has the potential to change their preferences or actual purchase behaviour.

Source: Gao, L., Melero-Polo, I. & Sese, F. J. (2020). Customer Equity Drivers, Customer Experience Quality, and Customer Profitability in Banking Services: The Moderating Role of Social Influence. *Journal of Service Research*, 23(2), 174-193.

Social loafing

Definition: Social loafing is a phenomenon that individuals tend to put in less effort when working collectively than individually.

Source: Chang, Y., Hou, R.-J., Wang, K., Cui, A. P. & Zhang, C.-B. (2020). Effects of intrinsic and extrinsic motivation on social loafing in online travel communities. *Computers in Human Behavior*, 109, 106360.

Social marketing

Definition: Social marketing is defined as marketing activities through social networks.

Source: Vahdati, Y. & Voss Kevin, E. (2019). Brand identification, cause-brand alliances and perceived cause controversy. *Journal of Product & Brand Management*, 28(7), 880-892.

Social Media

Definition (1): Social media is defined as a group of Internet-based applications that build on the ideological and technological foundations of Web 2.0, and that allow the creation and exchange of User Generated Content.

> **Source:** Sitta, D., Faulkner, M. & Stern, P. (2018). What can the brand manager expect from Facebook? *Australasian Marketing Journal (AMJ), 26*(1), 17-22.

Definition (2): Social media can be defined as online applications, platforms and media which aim to facilitate interactions, collaborations and the sharing of contents.

> **Source:** Dabbous, A. & Barakat, K. A. (2020). Bridging the online offline gap: Assessing the impact of brands' social network content quality on brand awareness and purchase intention. *Journal of Retailing and Consumer Services, 53*, 101966.

Definition (3): Social media are digital platforms on which users can connect with other users, generate and distribute content, and engage in interactive communication.

> **Source:** Carpentier, M., Van Hoye, G. & Weijters, B. (2019). Attracting applicants through the organization's social media page: Signaling employer brand personality. *Journal of Vocational Behavior, 115*, 103326.

Social media analytics

Definition: Social media analytics is concerned with developing and evaluating informatics tools and frameworks to collect, monitor, analyze, summarize, and visualize social media data in order to facilitate conversations and interactions to extract useful patterns and intelligence.

> **Source:** Garg, P., Gupta, B., Dzever, S., Sivarajah, U. & Kumar, V. (2020). Examining the Relationship between Social Media Analytics Practices and Business Performance in the Indian Retail and IT Industries: The Mediation Role of Customer Engagement. *International Journal of Information Management, 52*, 102069.

Social network

Definition: Social network has been defined as a specific set of linkages among a defined set of persons, groups and business bodies.

> **Source:** Zhang, L. & Zhang, J. (2018). Perception of small tourism enterprises in Lao PDR regarding social sustainability under the influence of social network. *Tourism Management, 69*, 109-120.

Social presence

Definition: Social presence is defined as the awareness of communicating with another person or entity and has been conceptualized as the extent to which the communication is perceived as personal, friendly, and sociable.

> Source: Source: Carpentier, M., Van Hoye, G. & Weijters, B. (2019). Attracting applicants through the organization's social media page: Signaling employer brand personality. *Journal of Vocational Behavior, 115*, 103326.

Social rejection

Definition: Social rejection is defined as rejection originating from social others, such as individuals and social groups, and targeting the self or in-groups.

> Source: Hu, M., Qiu, P., Wan, F. & Stillman, T. (2018). Love or hate, depends on who's saying it: How legitimacy of brand rejection alters brand preferences. *Journal of Business Research, 90*, 164-170.

Social signaling value

Definition: Social signaling value of a category refers to the capability of certain products to signal a person's social status.

> Source: Mandler, T., Bartsch, F. & Han, C. M. (2020). Brand credibility and marketplace globalization: The role of perceived brand globalness and localness. *Journal of International Business Studies*.

Social visibility of brand consumption

Definition: Social visibility of brand consumption can be defined as the individual consumer's perception that the consumption experience with a certain brand is socially visible to and highly regarded by reference groups such as friends, family, and colleagues.

> Source: Source: So, K. K. F., Wu, L., Xiong, L. & King, C. (2018). Brand Management in the Era of Social Media: Social Visibility of Consumption and Customer Brand Identification. *Journal of Travel Research, 57*(6), 727-742.

Social-adjustive

Definition: Social-adjustive function is defined as a tendency to purchase and use brands to gain approval in social situations and to maintain relationships.

> Source: Schade, M., Hegner, S., Horstmann, F. & Brinkmann, N. (2016). The impact of attitude functions on luxury brand consumption: An age-based group comparison. *Journal of Business Research, 69*(1), 314-322.

Source credibility

Definition: Source credibility refers to the credibility of the communicator and has been defined as a communicator's positive characteristics that affect the receiver's acceptance of a message. Source credibility has been conceptualized as having two main dimensions—trustworthiness and expertise

Source: Zhang, B., Ritchie, B., Mair, J. & Driml, S. (2019). Is the Airline Trustworthy? The Impact of Source Credibility on Voluntary Carbon Offsetting. *Journal of Travel Research*, 58(5), 715-731.

Source expertness

Definition: Source expertness is defined as the extent to which the source is perceived to be a source of valid assertions. Moreover, source attractiveness is also defined as the degree to which the source is considered to be familiar, likeable, similar and attractive.

Source: Cuomo, M., Foroudi, P., Tortora, D., Hussain, S. & Melewar, T. C. (2019). Celebrity Endorsement and the Attitude Towards Luxury Brands for Sustainable Consumption. *Sustainability*, 11, 6791.

Spillover

Definition: Spillover effect refers to the phenomenon in which an event influences beliefs regarding attributes that are not directly associated with the event itself.

Source: Fan, B., Li, C. & Jin, J. (2019). The Brand Scandal Spillover Effect at the Country Level: Evidence From Event-Related Potentials. *Frontiers in Neuroscience*, 13.

Sponsorship

Definition: Sponsorship has been defined as a cash and/or in-kind fee paid to a property (sports, entertainment, non-profit event or organization) in return for access to the exploitable commercial potential associated with that property.

Source: Zhu, H., Li, Q. & Liao, J. (2018). Doing well when doing good: the fit between corporate sponsorship and brand concept. *Journal of Consumer Marketing*, 35(7), 733-742.

Static appearance

Definition: Static appearance dimension involves consumers' perceptions towards static aspects of employees' embodied presentation, whereas the performative mannerisms dimension includes perceptions of employees' dynamic performance in service encounters.

Source: Wu, L., King, C. A., Lu, L. & Guchait, P. (2020). Hospitality aesthetic labor management: Consumers' and prospective employees' perspectives of hospitality brands. *International Journal of Hospitality Management*, 87, 102373.

Status consumption

Definition: Status consumption is defined as the motivational process by which individuals strive to improve their social standing through the conspicuous consumption of consumer products that confer and symbolize status both for the individual and surrounding.

> Source: Bazi, S., Filieri, R. & Gorton, M. (2020). Customers' motivation to engage with luxury brands on social media. *Journal of Business Research*, 112, 223-235.

Stimulus

Definition: Stimulus is considered to be environmental cues that affect the emotional state of the consumers.

> Source: Min, J. H. J., Chang, H. J. J., Jai, T.-M. C. & Ziegler, M. (2019). The effects of celebrity-brand congruence and publicity on consumer attitudes and buying behavior. *Fashion and Textiles*, 6(1), 10.

Stimulus-organism-response

Definition: Stimulus-organism-response is a theoretical model the encompasses, environmental stimuli (S) which generates an emotional or cognitive reaction (O) which, in turn, drives consumers' behavioral response (R).

> Source: Dabbous, A. & Barakat, K. A. (2020). Bridging the online offline gap: Assessing the impact of brands' social network content quality on brand awareness and purchase intention. *Journal of Retailing and Consumer Services*, 53, 101966.

Store image

Definition: Store image refers to the physical attractiveness of the atmosphere or environment of a store and it can be defined as a cognition and/or affect (or a set of cognitions and/or affects).

> Source: Massara, F., Scarpi, D., Melara, R. D. & Porcheddu, D. (2018). Affect transfer from national brands to store brands in multi-brand stores. *Journal of Retailing and Consumer Services*, 45, 103-110.

Sub brand

Definition: Sub-brand refers to products for which a new brand name is added adjacent to an existing brand name (e.g. Gillette Venus, Macintosh Quadra).

> Source: Azar Salim, L., Aimé, I. & Ulrich, I. (2018). Brand gender-bending: The impact of an endorsed brand strategy on consumers' evaluation of gendered mixed-target brands. *European Journal of Marketing*, 52(7/8), 1598-1624.

Subcultural

Definition: Subcultural is associated with an autonomous group of people who are perceived to operate independent from outside of mainstream society.

> Source: Warren, C., Batra, R., Loureiro, S. M. C. & Bagozzi, R. P. (2019). Brand Coolness. *Journal of Marketing*, 83(5), 36-56.

Subcultural brand

Definition: Subcultural brand is associated with an autonomous group of people who are perceived to operate independent from and outside of mainstream society.

> **Source:** Warren, C., Batra, R., Loureiro, S. M. C. & Bagozzi, R. P. (2019). Brand Coolness. *Journal of Marketing*, 83(5), 36-56.

Subjective norm

Definition: Subjective norm is defined as the perceived social pressure to perform or not to perform the behavior.

> **Source:** Sijoria, C., Mukherjee, S. & Datta, B. (2018). Impact of the antecedents of eWOM on CBBE. *Marketing Intelligence & Planning*, 36(5), 528-542.

Susceptibility of normative influence

Definition: Susceptibility of normative influence is the need to identify or enhance one's image with significant others through the acquisition and use of products and brands, the willingness to conform to the expectations of others regarding purchase decisions.

> **Source:** Kelley James, B. & Alden Dana, L. (2016). Online brand community: through the eyes of Self-Determination Theory. *Internet Research*, 26(4), 790-808.

Symbolic meaning

Definition: Symbolic meaning of a brand derives from the associations between the brand, its typical users, and its uses.

> **Source:** Gaustad, T., Utgård, J. & Fitzsimons, G. J. (2020). When accidents are good for a brand. *Journal of Business Research*, 107, 153-161.

Tie strength

Definition: Tie strength refers to the potency of the bond between members of a network. The connections with family members and close friends are tighter and stronger than those among acquaintances, colleagues, and classmates.

> **Source:** Wang, T., Yeh, R. K.-J., Chen, C. & Tsydypov, Z. (2016). What drives electronic word-of-mouth on social networking sites? Perspectives of social capital and self-determination. *Telematics and Informatics*, 33(4), 1034-1047.

Trust

Definition (1): Trust is a psychological state comprising the intention to accept vulnerability based upon positive expectations of the intentions or behavior of another.

Source: Yakimova, R., Owens, M. & Sydow, J. (2019). Formal control influence on franchisee trust and brand-supportive behavior within franchise networks. *Industrial Marketing Management, 76*, 123-135.

Definition (2): Trust has been defined as affect-based, referring to a feeling that is the outcome of a communal relationship with a brand.

Source: Baumann, C., Hamin, H. & Chong, A. (2015). The role of brand exposure and experience on brand recall—Product durables vis-à-vis FMCG. *Journal of Retailing and Consumer Services, 23*, 21-31.

Definition (3): Trust is defined as the willingness to rely on an exchange partner in whom one has confidence. Trust also relates to the perceived credibility and benevolence of the firm rendering the service.

Source: Agyei, J., Sun, S., Abrokwah, E., Penney, E. K. & Ofori-Boafo, R. (2020). Influence of Trust on Customer Engagement: Empirical Evidence From the Insurance Industry in Ghana. *SAGE Open, 10*(1), 2158244019899104.

Definition (4): Trust can be defined as the belief in the trustworthiness of the partner and the willingness to rely on him/her in a situation of vulnerability.

Source: Langaro, D., de Fátima Salgueiro, M., Rita, P. & Del Chiappa, G. (2019). Users' Participation in Facebook Brand Pages and Its Influence on Word-of-Mouth: The Role of Brand Knowledge and Brand Relationship. *Journal of Creative Communications*,

Trustworthiness

Definition (1): Trustworthiness is defined as the extent to which the stakeholder is confident about the brand.

Source: Merz, M. A., Zarantonello, L. & Grappi, S. (2018). How valuable are your customers in the brand value co-creation process? The development of a Customer Co-Creation Value (CCCV) scale. *Journal of Business Research, 82*, 79-89.

Definition (2): Trustworthiness is defined as the degree of confidence in the communicator's intent to communicate the assertions he considers most valid.

Source: Zhang, B., Ritchie, B., Mair, J. & Driml, S. (2019). Is the Airline Trustworthy? The Impact of Source Credibility on Voluntary Carbon Offsetting. *Journal of Travel Research, 58*(5), 715-731.

Underdog brands and top dog brands

Definition: Underdog brand is defined as a brand loser or predicted loser in a struggle or contest. Topdog brands refer to a brand in a position of authority especially through victory in a hard-fought competition.

Source: Kao Danny, T. & Wu, P.-H. (2019). The impact of affective orientation on bank preference as moderated by cognitive load and brand story style. *International Journal of Bank Marketing, 37*(5), 1334-1349.

Unfollowers brand page

Definition: Unfollowers, who are defined as individuals who stop following brand fans pages after their initial following decisions.

Source: Tang, Z., Chen, L. & Gillenson, M. L. (2019). Understanding brand fan page followers' discontinuance motivations: A mixed-method study. *Information & Management, 56*(1), 94-108.

Uniqueness

Definition: Uniqueness is defined as the degree to which consumers feel that a brand is different from competing brands (how distinct it is relative to competitors)

Source: Pourazad, N., Stocchi, L. & Pare, V. (2019). Brand attribute associations, emotional consumer-brand relationship and evaluation of brand extensions. *Australasian Marketing Journal (AMJ), 27*(4), 249-260.

Utilitarian function

Definition: Utilitarian function relates to the quality of goods and focuses on rational purposes. It is concerned with how a brand performs a desired product- or service-related function.

Source: Schade, M., Hegner, S., Horstmann, F. & Brinkmann, N. (2016). The impact of attitude functions on luxury brand consumption: An age-based group comparison. *Journal of Business Research, 69*(1), 314-322.

Utilitarian motivation

Definition: Utilitarian motivation is defined as rational and goal oriented, and it relates to effectiveness and instrumental value.

Source: Dabbous, A. & Barakat, K. A. (2020). Bridging the online offline gap: Assessing the impact of brands' social network content quality on brand awareness and purchase intention. *Journal of Retailing and Consumer Services, 53*, 101966.

Value co-creation

Definition: value co-creation implies a process of active interaction between the firm and its customers in order to create value. This value creation is centred on improving the customer's experience.

Source: González-Mansilla, Ó., Berenguer-Contrí, G. & Serra-Cantallops, A. (2019). The impact of value co-creation on hotel brand equity and customer satisfaction. *Tourism Management, 75*, 51-65.

Value equity
Definition: Value equity refers to the customers' objective assessment of the utility of a brand based on perceptions of what is given up for what is received.

> **Source:** Gao, L., Melero-Polo, I. & Sese, F. J. (2020). Customer Equity Drivers, Customer Experience Quality, and Customer Profitability in Banking Services: The Moderating Role of Social Influence. *Journal of Service Research, 23*(2), 174-193.

Value-congruity
Definition: Value-congruity is the customers' perceptual matching between their values and the brand values.

> **Source:** Kumar, J. & Nayak Jogendra, K. (2019). Brand engagement without brand ownership: a case of non-brand owner community members. *Journal of Product & Brand Management, 28*(2), 216-230.

Value-expressive features
Definition: Value-expressive features are brand characteristics that consumers typically use to express their personal values or images.

> **Source:** Sop, S. A. & Kozak, N. (2019). Effects of brand personality, self-congruity and functional congruity on hotel brand loyalty. *Journal of Hospitality Marketing & Management, 28*(8), 926-956.

Value-expressive function
Definition: A value-expressive function is defined as a tendency to purchase and use brands to communicate one's self-identity (beliefs, attitudes, values) to others.

> **Source:** Schade, M., Hegner, S., Horstmann, F. & Brinkmann, N. (2016). The impact of attitude functions on luxury brand consumption: An age-based group comparison. *Journal of Business Research, 69*(1), 314-322.

Value-expressive utility
Definition: Value-expressive utility refers to the hedonic benefits that a brand offers. Specifically, it refers to the fantasy, fun, and other hedonic associations of a brand.

> **Source:** Davari, A., Iyer, P. & Guzmán, F. (2017). Determinants of brand resurrection movements: Why consumers want dead brands back? *European Journal of Marketing, 51*(11/12), 1896-1917.

Warmth

Definition: Warmth is felt when one perceives another to have good intentions, and competence is felt when one perceives another to have the ability to carry out those intentions.

> **Source:** Portal, S., Abratt, R. & Bendixen, M. (2018). Building a human brand: Brand anthropomorphism unravelled. *Business Horizons*, 61(3), 367-374.

Web 2.0

Definition: Web 2.0 technology is defined as a new (online) communication platform that transforms traditional communication attitudes to online communication. Web 2.0 technologies allow users to share content which is created by them.

> **Source:** Sagynbekova, S., Ince, E., Ogunmokun, O. A., Olaoke, R. O. & Ukeje, U. E. (2020) Social media communication and higher education brand equity: The mediating role of eWOM. *Journal of Public Affairs*.

Website interativity

Definition: Website interactivity is one of the most essential design components in any commercial website and website interactivity helps a company to communicate its brand messages to Internet users.

> **Source:** Barreda, A. A., Bilgihan, A., Nusair, K. & Okumus, F. (2016). Online branding: Development of hotel branding through interactivity theory. *Tourism Management*, 57, 180-192.

Willingness to sacrifice

Definition: Willingness to sacrifice refers to the degree to which an individual is willing to make sacrifices to continue their relationship with the brand.

> **Source:** Grace, D., Ross, M. & King, C. (2018). Brand fidelity: a relationship maintenance perspective. *Journal of Brand Management*, 25(6), 577-590.

Willingness to try a brand

Definition: Wilingness to try a brand refers to consumers' willingness to use the product without previous experiences with the brand.

> **Source:** Southworth Sarah, S. & Ha-Brookshire, J. (2016). The impact of cultural authenticity on brand uniqueness and willingness to try: The case of Chinese brands and US consumers. *Asia Pacific Journal of Marketing and Logistics*, 28(4), 724-742.

Word of mouth

Definition (1): Word of mouth is the information and/or rumor sharing between individuals and this influence of conversations between people is higher than the influence of traditional media or advertising.

Source: Swani, K. & Milne, G. R. (2017). Evaluating Facebook brand content popularity for service versus goods offerings. *Journal of Business Research, 79,* 123-133.

Definition (2): Word of mouth is defined as the process through which informal and non-commercially intended information is exchanged between a communicator and a receiver about a brand, service or organisation.

Source: Langaro, D., de Fátima Salgueiro, M., Rita, P. & Del Chiappa, G. (2019). Users' Participation in Facebook Brand Pages and Its Influence on Word-of-Mouth: The Role of Brand Knowledge and Brand Relationship. *Journal of Creative Communications,* 14(3), 177-195

INDEX

ACTIVATION	1
ACTIVE BRAND LOGO	1
ACTIVE BRAND PERSONALITY	1
ACTIVE ENGAGEMENT	1
ACTUAL SELF	1
AD SKEPTICISM	1
AESTHETIC	2
AESTHETIC LABOR FIT PERCEPTIONS	2
AESTHETICALLY APPEALING	2
AFFECT	2
AFFECTION	3
AFFECTIVE BRAND TRUST	3
AFFECTIVE EXPERIENCE	3
AFFECTIVE ORIENTATION	3
AGREEABLENESS	3
ALTRUISM	3
AMBASSADOR BEHAVIORS	4
ANIMOSITY	4
ANTHROPOMORPHISM	4
ARTIFICIAL INTELLIGENCE	5
ATTACHMENT	5
ATTITUDE	5
ATTITUDE TOWARD A BRAND	6
ATTITUDES TOWARD FOREIGN PRODUCTS	6
ATTITUDINAL LOYALTY	6
ATTRIBUTION THEORY	7
AUTHENTIC BRAND	7
AUTOBIOGRAPHICAL MEMORIES	7
B2B BRAND	7
BEHAVIORAL BRAND LOYALTY	7
BEHAVIORAL EXPERIENCE	7
BEHAVIORAL INVOLVEMENT	8
BEHAVIORAL LOYALTY	8
BENEVOLENCE	8
BRAND	8
BRAND ACQUAINTANCING	9
BRAND ACTIVATION	10
BRAND ADDICTION	10
BRAND ADMIRATION	10
BRAND ADVOCACY	10
BRAND AESTHETIC	10
BRAND AFECTION	11
BRAND AFFECT	11
BRAND AFFILIATION	11
BRAND AFFINITY	11
BRAND AGE	11
BRAND ALIGNMENT	12
BRAND ALLIANCE	12
BRAND AMBASSADOR	12
BRAND AMBASSADOR PROGRAM	12
BRAND ANTHROPOMORPHISM	12
BRAND ANTHROPOMORPHIZATION	13
BRAND APP RESISTANCE	13
BRAND APPEAL	13
BRAND ARCHITECTURE	13
BRAND ASSOCIATIONS	14
BRAND ATRIBUTES	14
BRAND ATTACHMENT	15
BRAND ATTACK	15
BRAND ATTITUDE	16
BRAND ATTITUDE CHANGE	16
BRAND ATTRACTIVENESS	16

BRAND ATTRIBUTE ASSOCIATION............16	BRAND CONSTELLATION 25
BRAND AURA......................16	BRAND COOLNESS...................25
BRAND AUTHENTICITY.................16	BRAND CREATIVITY 25
BRAND AVOIDANCE.................18	BRAND CREDIBILITY...............26
BRAND AWARENESS 18	BRAND CRISIS 26
BRAND BELIEF................18	BRAND CULTURE 27
BRAND BENEFITS...................19	BRAND CULTURAL SYMBOLISM 27
BRAND BENEVOLENCE 19	BRAND DELETION 27
BRAND BIOGRAPHIES 19	BRAND DIFFERENTIATION 27
BRAND BUILDING BEHAVIOR 19	BRAND DILUTION 28
BRAND CENTRED CONTROL...............19	BRAND DIS-IDENTIFICATION 28
BRAND CHAMPION..................20	BRAND DISTINCTIVENESS...............28
BRAND CHARACTER..................20	BRAND EFFECT 28
BRAND CHARACTERISTIC 20	BRAND ELEGANCE..............28
BRAND CHARISMA....................20	BRAND ELEMENTS 29
BRAND CHOICE ATTAINMENT 20	BRAND EMBARRASSMENT................29
BRAND CITIZENSHIP BEHAVIOR.............21	BRAND EMOTION 29
BRAND CLARITY 21	BRAND ENDORSEMENT..............29
BRAND CO-CREATION..................21	BRAND ENERGY 30
BRAND CO-CREATION ENGAGEMENT 21	BRAND ENGAGEMENT.................30
BRAND CODE 22	BRAND ENGAGEMENT PLATFORM..........31
BRAND COMMITMENT 22	BRAND ENTHUSIASM..............31
BRAND COMMUNICATION 22	BRAND ENTIFICATION 31
BRAND COMMUNITY 22	BRAND ENTRETAINMENT CONTENT 31
BRAND COMMUNITY IDENTIFICATION ..23	BRAND EQUITY................31
BRAND COMPASS 23	BRAND ETHEREALITY 34
BRAND COMPATIBILITY 23	BRAND ETHICALITY 34
BRAND COMPETENCE.................24	BRAND EVALUATIONS.................34
BRAND COMPETITIVENESS 24	BRAND EVANGELISM 34
BRAND CONCEPT 24	BRAND EXCLUSIVITY 35
BRAND CONNECTION 24	BRAND EXPERIENCE 35
BRAND CONSCIOUSNESS................24	BRAND EXPERIENTIAL SATISFACTION ..35
BRAND CONSISTENCY....................25	BRAND EXPERTISE................36

BRAND EXPOSURE 36	BRAND INTEGRATION 43
BRAND EXTENSION 36	BRAND INTEGRITY 44
BRAND FAILURE 36	BRAND INTERACTIVITY 44
BRAND FAMILIARITY 36	BRAND INTEREST 44
BRAND FAN PAGE 37	BRAND INTIMACY 44
BRAND FAN PAGE DISCONTINUANCE 37	BRAND INVOLVEMENT 44
BRAND FEELINGS 37	BRAND JEALOUSY 45
BRAND FIDELITY 37	BRAND KNOWLEDGE 45
BRAND FIT 37	BRAND LEGITIMACY 45
BRAND FORGIVENESS 38	BRAND LICENSING 46
BRAND FUNCTIONAL CONGRUITY 38	BRAND LOCALNESS 46
BRAND FUNCTIONALITY 38	BRAND LOGO 46
BRAND GENDER 38	BRAND LONGEVITY 46
BRAND GENDER PERCEPTION CHANGE. 39	BRAND LOVE 47
BRAND GENERICIZATION 39	BRAND LOYALTY 47
BRAND GLOBALITY 39	BRAND LUXURIOUSNESS 48
BRAND GLOBALNESS 39	BRAND MANAGEMENT EFFICIENCY 48
BRAND GOAL-CONGRUENCE 39	BRAND MASCOT 49
BRAND GOODWILL 39	BRAND MEANING 49
BRAND GOVERNANCE 40	BRAND MIANZI 49
BRAND HAPPINESS 40	BRAND MICROBLOG 49
BRAND HATE 40	BRAND MICRO-BLOG IDENTIFICATION.. 49
BRAND HERITAGE 40	BRAND NARRATIVE 50
BRAND HIGH STATUS 41	BRAND NEED FOR COGNITION 50
BRAND HYPOCRISY 41	BRAND NEWS 50
BRAND ICON 41	BRAND NOSTALGIA 50
BRAND IDENTIFICATION 41	BRAND ORIENTATION 50
BRAND IDENTITY 41	BRAND ORIGIN 51
BRAND IMAGE 41	BRAND PAGE 51
BRAND IMAGE CONGRUITY 42	BRAND PAGE ACTIVITY 51
BRAND IMITATION 43	BRAND PAGE COMMITMENT 51
BRAND INNER SELF EXPRESSIVENESS ... 43	BRAND PAGE CONTENT QUALITY 52
BRAND INNOVATIVENESS 43	BRAND PAGE INTERACTIVITY 52

BRAND PASSION	52	BRAND RELATIONSHIP	59
BRAND PENETRATION	52	BRAND RELATIONSHIP QUALITY	59
BRAND PERCEPTIONS	53	BRAND RELATIONSHIP QUALITY	59
BRAND PERFORMANCE	53	BRAND RELATIONSHIP STRENGTH	60
BRAND PERSONALITY	53	BRAND RELIGIOSITY	60
BRAND PLACEMENT	53	BRAND REPUTATION	60
BRAND PLACEMENT STRENGTH	54	BRAND RESONANCE	61
BRAND PLAY	54	BRAND RESPECT	61
BRAND POLARIZATION	54	BRAND RESPONSES	61
BRAND POPULARITY	54	BRAND RESURRECTION MOVEMENT	62
BRAND PORTFOLIO	54	BRAND RETAILER	62
BRAND PORTFOLIO COHERENCE	54	BRAND REVITALIZATION	62
BRAND PORTFOLIO FIT	55	BRAND RIVALRY	62
BRAND PORTFOLIO STRENGTH	55	BRAND ROMANCE	62
BRAND POSITIONING	55	BRAND SALIENCE	63
BRAND POST	55	BRAND SATISFACTION	63
BRAND POWER	55	BRAND SCANDAL	63
BRAND PREDICTABILITY	56	BRAND SCARCITY	63
BRAND PREFERENCE	56	BRAND SCHEMATA	63
BRAND PRESTIGE	56	BRAND SCHEMATICITY	63
BRAND PRIDE	56	BRAND SCORE	64
BRAND PROMINENCE	56	BRAND SELF CONNECTION	64
BRAND PROMISE	57	BRAND SELF-RELEVANCE	64
BRAND PROTOTYPE	57	BRAND SENSITIVITY	64
BRAND PSYCHOLOGICAL OWNERSHIP	57	BRAND SENTIMENT	64
BRAND PUBLIC	57	BRAND SIGNATURE	65
BRAND QUALITY	57	BRAND SKILLS	65
BRAND RECALL	58	BRAND SKILLS	65
BRAND RECOGNITION	58	BRAND SOCIAL NETWORKS NARRATIVES	65
BRAND RECOVERY	58	BRAND SOCIAL RESPONSIBILITY	65
BRAND REGENERATION	59	BRAND SOCIAL SELF-EXPRESSIVENESS	66
BRAND REGRET	59	BRAND SPECIFIC TRANSFORMATIONAL LEADERSHIP	66
BRAND REJECTION	59		

BRAND SPECIFIC TRANSACTIONAL LEADERSHIP 66	BRANDING 74
BRAND STABILITY 66	BRAND-POST CONGRUENCE 74
BRAND STATUS 66	BRAND–RETAILER–CHANNEL AWARENESS 74
BRAND STEREOTYPE 67	BRAND–RETAILER–CHANNEL CONSUMER LOYALTY 74
BRAND STORY 67	
BRAND STORY TRANSPORTATION 67	BRAND–RETAILER–CHANNEL PERCEIVED QUALITY 75
BRAND STORYTELLING 67	
BRAND STRENGTH 67	BUSINESS PERFORMANCE 75
BRAND SUCCESS 68	CAUSE RELATED MARKETING 75
BRAND SUPERIORITY 68	CAUSE-BRAND ALLIANCE 75
BRAND SUPPORTIVE INTENTIONS 68	CBBE (CUSTOMER BASED BRAND EQUITY) 75
BRAND SURFEITS 68	CELEBRITY 76
BRAND SUSTAINABILITY 68	CELEBRITY CREDIBILITY 76
BRAND SYMBOLISM 69	CELBRITY ENDORSER 76
BRAND SYNONYMITY 69	CELEBRITY ENDORSEMENTS 76
BRAND TARNISHMENT 69	CELEBRITY IMAGE 77
BRAND TRANSFORMATION 69	CHANNEL EQUITY 77
BRAND TRANSGRESSION 69	CHATBOTS 77
BRAND TRIBALISM 70	CITY ATTACHMENT 77
BRAND TRIBE 70	CITY BRAND AMBASSADORSHIP BEHAVIOR 77
BRAND TRUST 70	
BRAND TRUSTWORTHINESS 71	CITY BRAND EXPERIENCE 77
BRAND TRUTH 71	CO-BRANDING 78
BRAND UNDERSTANDING 72	CO-CREATION 78
BRAND UNIQUENESS 72	COGNITION 78
BRAND VALUE 72	COGNITIVE BRAND TRUST 78
BRAND VALUES 72	COGNITIVE LOAD 79
BRAND VARIANT 73	COGNITIVE LOYALTY 79
BRAND VISION 73	COGNITIVE MANIFESTATIONS OF BRAND FIDELITY 79
BRAND WORK 73	
BRANDED COMMUNITY 73	COGNITIVE PROCESSING 79
BRANDED EMOTICON 73	COMMERCIAL SPONSORSHIP 79
BRANDED MERCHANDISE 74	COMMITMENT 79

COMMUNITY CITIZENSHIP BEHAVIOUR 80	COUNTRY OF ORIGIN IMAGE 86
COMMUNITY IDENTIFICATION 80	CREDIBILITY 86
COMPATIBILITY 80	CREDIBILITY OF A BRAND 86
COMPLAINT 80	CUSTOMER BRAND SATISFACTION 87
CONATIVE BRAND LOYALTY 81	CUSTOMER BRAND ENGAGEMENT 87
CONGRUENCY 81	CUSTOMER BRAND IDENTIFICATION 87
CONGRUITY 81	CUSTOMER CITIZENSHIP BEHAVIOR 88
CONNECTEDNESS 81	CUSTOMER ENGAGEMENT 88
CONSCIENTIOUSNESS 81	CUSTOMER EQUITY 88
CONSUMER EMPOWERMENT 81	CUSTOMER ETHNOCENTRISM 89
CONSUMER ETHNOCENTRISM 82	CUSTOMER EXPERIENCE 89
CONSUMER ONLINE ENGAGEMENT LEVEL 82	CUSTOMER EXPERIENCE QUALITY 89
	CUSTOMER LIFETIME VALUE 89
CONSUMER PERSUASION KNOWLEDGE . 82	CUSTOMER PARTICIPATION 90
CONSUMER VANITY 82	CUSTOMER PROFITABILITY 90
CONSUMER-BRAND ENGAGEMENT 82	CUSTOMER REFERRAL PROGRAMS 90
CONSUMER-BRAND IDENTIFICATION 83	CUSTOMER-BASED BRAND EQUITY, ... 90
CONSUMER-PERCEIVED BRAND AUTHENTICITY 83	CUSTOMER-BRAND IDENTIFICATION 90
CONSUMERS BRAND CREDIBILITY 83	CUSTOMIZATION 91
CONSUMERS' BRAND EVALUATIONS 83	CUTENESS 91
CONSUMERS' ENDURING CULTURAL INVOLVEMENT 84	DESIGN QUALITY 91
	DESIRE FOR RECONCILIATION 91
CONSUMER EXPERTISE 84	DESIRE FOR UNIQUE PRODUCTS 91
CONSUMPTION COLLECTIVES 84	DESTINATION BRANDING 92
CONTENT QUALITY 84	DYNAMIC BRAND LOGO 92
CONTINUANCE INTENTION TO FOLLOW 84	EASE OF USE 92
	EFFICIENCY 92
CONVENIENCE 85	ELECTRONIC WORD OF MOUTH 92
CONVERSATIONAL HUMAN VOICE 85	ELITISM 92
COPYCAT BRAND 85	EMOTIONAL BRAND ATTACHMENT 93
CORPORATE ASSOCIATIONS 85	EMOTIONAL BRAND ATTRACTION 93
CORPORATE BRAND 85	EMOTIONAL BRAND EXPERIENCE 93
CORPORATE SOCIAL RESPONSIBILITY 85	EMOTIONAL BRAND RELATIONSHIP 93
CORRESPONDENCE BIAS 86	

EMOTIONAL BRANDING 93	HEDONIC MOTIVATION 101
EMOTIONAL EXHAUSTION 94	HELPING BEHAVIOUR 101
EMPLOYEE BRAND EQUITY 94	HOMOPHILY 101
EMPLOYEES' STATIC APPEARANCE 94	HUMOR APPRECIATION 101
EMPLOYEES' VALUE CONGRUENCE 94	ICONIC BRAND 101
EMPLOYER BRAND EQUITY 94	IDEAL SELF 102
ENEGETIC BRAND 94	IMAGE 102
ENDORSER ATTRACTIVENESS 95	INFORMATION PROCESSING 102
ENDORSER BRAND CONGRUITY 95	INFORMATION QUALITY 102
ENDORSER ETHICALITY 95	INFORMATION QUANTITY 102
ENDORSER TRUSTWORTHINESS 95	INFORMATION USEFULNESS 102
ENDURING INVOLVEMENT 95	INFORMATIVENESS 103
ENERGETIC BRAND 96	INNOVATION ORIENTATION 103
ENTERTAINMENT 96	INTEGRITY 103
EVENT IMAGE 96	INTELLECTUAL EXPERIENCE 103
ELECTRONIC WORD OF MOUTH 96	INTERDEPENDENT SELF-CONSTRUAL 103
EXISTENTIAL AUTHENTICITY 96	INTERNAL BRANDING 103
EXTRAORDINARY BRAND 96	INTERPERSONAL INFLUENCE 104
FAMILIARITY 98	INTIMACY 104
FAMILY BUSINESS BRAND 98	INTRAPERSONAL AUTHENTICITY 105
FELT RESPONSIBILITY 98	INTRINSIC MOTIVATION 105
FIRM PRODUCT INNOVATION 98	INTUITIVE DECISION-MAKING 105
FRANCHISEE-BASED BRAND EQUITY 98	INVOLVEMENT 105
FRANCHISING 99	KINEMATIC BRAND LOGO 106
FUNCTIONAL BRAND QUALITIES 99	KNOWLEDGE 106
FUNCTIONAL UTILITY 99	LEGITIMACY 106
GLOBAL BRAND 99	LIFETIME VALUE METRIC 106
GREEN BRAND 100	LOCAL BRANDS 106
GREEN BRAND POSITIONING 100	LOGITUDINAL CONSISTENCY 107
HALO EFFECT 100	LOYALTY 107
HARMOUNIOUS PASSION 100	LUXURY BRAND 107
HATE 100	LUXURY CONSUMPTION TENDENCY 108
HEDONIC ATTRIBUTES 100	LUXURY PRODUCT 108

MARKET ORIENTATION 108	PERCEIVED SYSTEM QUALITY 114
MARKET PRESENCE 108	PERCEIVED USEFULNESS............................ 115
MATERIALISM 108	PERCEIVED VALUE 115
MODEL TTF - TASK-TECHNOLOGY FIT MODEL 109	PERFORMANCE RISK.................................... 115
MORAL IDENTITY... 109	PERSONAL CONTROL 116
NARCISSISM 109	PERSUASION KNOWLEDGE....................... 116
NARRATIVE FIDELITY................................. 109	PHILANTHROPIC SPONSORSHIP 116
NATIVE ADVERTISING 109	PLACE BRAND ATTACHMENT 116
NEGATIVE WORD OF MOUTH 110	PLACE BRAND.. 116
NON-VERBAL COMMUNICATION 110	PLACE SATISFACTION................................ 116
NOSTALGIA... 110	POLITICAL BRAND....................................... 117
OMNICHANNEL 110	POPULAR BRAND 117
ONLINE BRAND COMMUNITY 110	POWER.. 117
OPENNESS TO EXPERIENCE 111	PRESENTED BRAND.................................... 117
OPINION LEADERS....................................... 111	PRICE CONSCIOUSNESS............................. 117
ORIGINAL ATTRIBUTE................................ 111	PRIVATE LABELS 118
ORIGINAL BRAND.. 111	PROCESS INNOVATION.............................. 118
OVERALL BRAND EQUITY......................... 111	PROCESSING FLUENCY.............................. 118
PARA-SOCIAL INTERACTION.................... 111	PRODUCT CATEGORY INVOLVEMENT.. 118
PASSION 112	PRODUCT DESIGN APPEAL........................ 118
PERCEIVED BEHAVIOURAL........................ 112	PRODUCT INVOLVEMENT'S EFFICACY. 118
PERCEIVED BRAND GLOBALNESS 112	PRODUCT PLACEMENT 119
PERCEIVED BRAND LOCALNESS............. 112	PRODUCT-HARM CRISIS 119
PERCEIVED BRAND QUALITY 112	PSYCHOLOGICAL INVOLVEMENT 119
PERCEIVED FIT.. 112	PSYCHOLOGICAL WELL-BEING 119
PERCEIVED PLAYFULNESS........................ 113	PUBLIC-BASED EVALUATION 119
PERCEIVED PRIVACY................................... 113	PURCHASE INTENTION 120
PERCEIVED QUALITY 113	PURCHASE INVOLVEMENT 120
PERCEIVED RISK... 114	QUALITY COMMITMENT............................ 120
PERCEIVED SECURITY 114	RATIONAL DECISION MAKING................. 120
PERCEIVED SERVICE QUALITY................ 114	REBELLIOUS BRAND................................... 121
PERCEIVED STRENGTH OF BRAND ORIGIN 114	RELATEDNESS 121
	RELATIONAL BRAND ENGAGEMENT PLATFORMS 121

RELATIONSHIP COMMITMENT 121	SERVICE EXPERIENCE 128
RELATIONSHIP EQUITY 121	SERVICE FAILURE 128
RELIGION 121	SERVICE RECOVERY 128
REPURCHASE INTENTION 122	SHARED BRAND UNDERSTANDING 129
RESPONSIBLE BRAND PERSONALITY ... 122	SIGNALING THEORY 129
RETAILER EQUITY 122	SKILLS 129
RETAILER RELIABILITY 122	SLOGANS 129
RISK AVERSION 122	SOCIAL NETWORKS SERVICE ADVERTISING 129
ROLE THEORY 123	SOCIAL BENEFIT 130
SATISFACTION 123	SOCIAL IDENTITY THEORY 130
SCHEMA CONGRUITY 123	SOCIAL INFLUENCE 130
SECRET AFFAIRS WITH BRANDS 123	SOCIAL LOAFING 130
SELF-BASED EVALUATION 123	SOCIAL MARKETING 130
SELF CONGRUENCE 124	SOCIAL MEDIA 131
SELF EXPRESSIVE BRAND 124	SOCIAL MEDIA ANALYTICS 131
SELF-ACCEPTANCE' 124	SOCIAL NETWORK 131
SELF-BRAND CONNECTION 124	SOCIAL PRESENCE 131
SELF-BRAND IDENTIFICATION 125	SOCIAL REJECTION 132
SELF-BRAND INTEGRATION 125	SOCIAL SIGNALING VALUE 132
SELF-BRANDING 125	SOCIAL VISIBILITY OF BRAND CONSUMPTION 132
SELF-CONCEPT 125	SOCIAL-ADJUSTIVE 132
SELF-CONGRUENCY 126	SOURCE CREDIBILITY 132
SELF-CONGRUITY 126	SOURCE EXPERTNESS 133
SELF-CONNECTION 126	SPILLOVER 133
SELF-CONSCIOUSNESS 126	SPONSORSHIP 133
SELF-CONSISTENCY 126	STATIC APPEARANCE 133
SELF-CONSTRUAL THEORY 127	STATUS CONSUMPTION 133
SELF-DETERMINATION THEORY 127	STIMULUS 134
SELF-EFFICACY 127	STIMULUS-ORGANISM-RESPONSE 134
SELF-ESTEEM 127	STORE IMAGE 134
SELF-REASSURANCE 128	SUB BRAND 134
SENSORY EXPERIENCE 128	SUBCULTURAL 134
SENSORY MARKETING 128	

SUBCULTURAL BRAND 135	VALUE CO-CREATION 137
SUBJECTIVE NORM 135	VALUE EQUITY 138
SUSCEPTIBILITY OF NORMATIVE INFLUENCE 135	VALUE-CONGRUITY 138
	VALUE-EXPRESSIVE FEATURES 138
SYMBOLIC MEANING 135	VALUE-EXPRESSIVE FUNCTION 138
TIE STRENGTH 135	VALUE-EXPRESSIVE UTILITY 138
TRUST 135	WARMTH 139
TRUSTWORTHINESS 136	WEB 2.0 139
UNDERDOG BRANDS AND TOP DOG BRANDS 136	WEBSITE INTERATIVITY 139
	WILLINGNESS TO SACRIFICE 139
UNFOLLOWERS BRAND PAGE 137	WILLINGNESS TO TRY A BRAND 139
UNIQUENESS 137	WORD OF MOUTH 139
UTILITARIAN FUNCTION 137	
UTILITARIAN MOTIVATION 137	

www.ingramcontent.com/pod-product-compliance
Lightning Source LLC
Chambersburg PA
CBHW070640220526
45466CB00001B/243